Toward a Just Correctional System

Experiments in Implementing Democracy in Prisons

Joseph E. Hickey
Peter L. Scharf

Toward a Just Correctional System

 Jossey-Bass Publishers

San Francisco • Washington • London • 1980

TOWARD A JUST CORRECTIONAL SYSTEM
Experiments in Implementing Democracy in Prisons
by Joseph E. Hickey and Peter L. Scharf

Copyright © 1980 by: Jossey-Bass Inc., Publishers
433 California Street
San Francisco, California 94104
&
Jossey-Bass Limited
28 Banner Street
London EC1Y 8QE

Library of Congress Cataloging in Publication Data

Hickey, Joseph E
  Toward a just correctional system.

  Bibliography: p. 197
  Includes index.
  1. Corrections—United States. 2. Prisons—United
States. 3. Prisoners—Legal status, laws, etc.—United
States. I. Scharf, Peter, 1945–   joint author.
II. Title.
HV9304.H53   365'.973   79-88112
ISBN 0-87589-396-1

Manufactured in the United States of America

JACKET DESIGN BY WILLI BAUM

FIRST EDITION

Code 8015

The Jossey-Bass
Social and Behavioral Science Series

Preface

> The prison should, were the world not full of paradox, be a
> very paradigm of the rule of law.
> —Norval Morris, *Future of Imprisonment* (1974)

In a democratic society, the very idea of prison is a paradox—or rather
a series of paradoxes. After all, how can such a society ultimately
justify continuing to keep people, even prisoners, in a condition of
political and economic servitude? How can this society instill, in
people who have shown such fundamental disrespect for it, the sense
of democratic community that makes it work? How can the society
find a way to extend the democratic rights guaranteed other citizens to
those convicted of serious felonies?

Prisoners are the most powerless of people. Legally, historically, and in the popular mind, they are noncitizens, nonpersons.
From the society, they can demand nothing, not even minimal conditions of respect and safety. Why, then, *should* society extend them
democratic rights?

There are three justifications—philosophical, historical, and
psychological—for extending democratic ideals to the daily conduct
of the prison.

Philosophically, it can be argued that all human beings
deserve respect, no matter what they might have done to society or its

ix

members. It can also be argued that the prison's punitiveness and denial of prisoners' political and economic rights are simply not just, as might be suggested by Rawls (1971), who states the conditions under which he feels a just society may restrict liberty or permit equality in its citizens.

Historically, there has also existed an obscure but important movement to reform prisons by extending democratic process to prisoners. As we shall describe, Alexander Maconochie's mark system, Thomas Mott Osborne's Mutual Welfare League, and Eliot Studt's C unit study are representative of this tradition.

Psychologically, developmental psychology (as embodied in the works of such thinkers as George Herbert Mead, John Dewey, Jean Piaget, and Lawrence Kohlberg) offers a conception of learning that may be appropriate here. Kohlberg, for example, suggests that people evolve through six stages of ethical or moral development and that this moral development is stimulated by, among other things, participation in democratic life. Clearly, traditional prisons fail to provide an environment likely to allow such development.

On the basis of these premises, in 1970 we initiated, in collaboration with Harvard University, a small-scale effort in which prisoners engaged in democratic dialogue about management of living-unit discipline, recreation, and the like, in the hope of demonstrating that inmates would respond positively to such an environment and would recognize that its rules and procedures were fairer than were those in the traditional prison. In addition, we were interested in exploring the use of the Kohlberg measure of moral judgment as a tool for measuring democratic learning in the prison. We were also interested in the impact of such a democratic intervention on the political and social culture of the prison.

After a year of preliminary work, we launched a project to create a democratic prison environment that would, we hoped, be perceived as fair by inmates and staff and that would actively stimulate the moral thinking of the people involved. We also hoped the program would aid inmates in leading successful lives following their release from the institution. The Just Community program was initiated in 1971 at the Niantic Correctional Institution for Women in East Lyme, Connecticut. There had been a near riot at the institution, and feelings between staff and inmates were generally hostile. In spite of these antagonisms, inmates, staff, and administrators all expressed a willingness to explore the possibility of at least working together to create a new set of living unit rules. Inmates and staff members agreed to propose, institute, and enforce rules for a single "model cottage," as well as to work toward a positive sense of community. Implicit in this agreement was the recognition by prison administrators that inmates and line staff could legitimately discuss and attempt to restructure existing institutional arrangements.

Once operational, cottage meetings were held several times a week, and grievances, program suggestions, and parole and furlough petitions were brought up for open discussion by staff and inmates. Even such potentially explosive issues as contraband, escape, and assault were talked about in these meetings, and in only a few cases was a community decision directly overruled by the prison administration. Besides the meetings, residents also attended several weekly counseling sessions, led by trained cottage staff members, which had a more personal focus than did the larger meetings. In both encounters, inmates and staff were trained in methods of democratic management and discussion.

The Just Community program has lasted for eight years. In the following pages, we describe its background, methodology, procedures, its successes and failures, and, we hope, its ultimate justification. We realize that, in our supposedly pragmatic age, articulating a theory of prison reform that upholds an abstract notion of social justice runs the risk of sounding soft-headed and romantic. Others concerned with prisons may argue for "tough-minded" ways of "correcting the illusions" of rehabilitation and reform, citing promises of lowered recidivism. Our justification has little to do with lowered recidivism, although we hope it helps. Rather, we feel the reason to reform prisons stems from a commitment to social justice: That is, a just society should seek to guarantee social rights for *all* its people, and inmates simply should not be subjected to the degradations, cruelty, hopelessness, and despair that most experience in American prisons today. The right to democratic participation in prison is more than a psychological or educational technique; it is a fundamental political right. Further, we insist that, far from being soft-headed and romantic, the extension of rights to prisoners is the only way to ensure justice to all citizens, particularly the victims of crime.

Chapter One is an overview of three major historical efforts to create democratic prison programs. In reviewing the efforts of Maconochie, Osborne, and Studt, we emphasize both the promise as well as the constraints facing efforts at prison democracy. Historians interested in the evolution of criminal justice should find this chapter particularly rewarding since we have deliberately chosen three interveners who utilized self-government for different reasons at different times.

Chapter Two offers a conceptual rationale using psychological research as   philosophical criteria for the developmental reeducation of prison inmates. This research played a vital role in developing several classroom interventions, and our efforts at moral education among school-aged children served to expand our own technology in several areas. We have included several sample meetings illustrating our basic educational strategy for psychologists and educators concerned with the issue of moral education.

Chapters Three and Four outline our intervention project as it evolved through two phases. Initially, our self-governing units were conceived as rehabilitative instruments. It soon became clear, however, that prison reform was the more pressing issue if the democratic ideal was to be viable. The units, therefore, became laboratories that not only served inmates but also explored the inner workings of the prison. The inevitable conflicts between a minidemocracy and the larger bureaucratic autocracy served to sharpen the conceptual as well as the practical inconsistencies implicit in both prison management and bureaucracies generally—and we hope that this and subsequent chapters will provide political scientists with a fresh perspective on the human consequences of bureaucratic decision making.

Chapter Five describes in detail the community meetings and small group meetings of the project. Besides their educational value, they can serve as a basis for comparative group studies, thereby furthering theory integration in the clinical area.

Chapter Six, containing preliminary research results, deals with inmate perceptions of prison moral atmosphere and moral stage change during their participation in our democratic living units. While the findings are generally positive, they inevitably raise more questions than they resolve. We hope our work will spur others to pursue some of those areas.

Finally, Chapters Seven and Eight discuss the constraints we identified in the interaction of democracy within prison. We have attempted to report our findings and recommendations in such a way as to attract the interest of sociologists and political scientists familiar with the traditional literature on total institutions. We hope our views and recommendations will renew interest in the central question: How should a society that espouses democratic ideals undertake to punish its criminals? We argue that it can and should be done through the democratic process itself and offer what we believe to be a workable framework by which individual rights and responsibilities can be exercised. We await the reaction of the growing number of social philosophers concerned with the issue of human rights and legal ethics to our extension of the Rawlsian paradigm to prisoners.

We believe a complete rethinking of America's penal process is needed as never before. Such issues as victimology and victim compensation have gradually taken on new significance with little in the way of practical results. Similarly, the matter of prisoners' rights has lain dormant, perhaps reflective of the nation's general social malaise. It is time, it seems to us, to get on with the job of pursuing justice and restructuring our legal system accordingly. Toward that end, we would hope that legislators and administrators alike will consider our proposals carefully. Although we do not claim that our work is complete, we are confident that careful pilot applications will prove them worthwhile.

Acknowledgments

The work described herein represents the labors of numerous individuals. In the first few months of activity, for example, Lawrence Kohlberg and Joseph Hickey collaborated on the design and implementation of the Cheshire group intervention. Later Douglas Freundlich and Peter Scharf, then doctoral candidates at Harvard, helped with the group meetings as well as the conceptual work of the democratic component. The early efforts at Niantic fell to Hickey and Scharf with the support of Kohlberg. At this point numerous people both within the Connecticut Department of Corrections and at Harvard University played vital roles. While training and advisory work to the Niantic staff was provided by a Harvard team coordinated by the authors, day-to-day operations were the responsibility of Niantic personnel.

In early 1972 Hickey joined the staff of the Connecticut Department of Corrections central office, partly to ease the financial burden on an already overextended Harvard budget. This permitted several new Harvard people to examine the experimental unit from various disciplinary viewpoints and added immeasurably to the theoretical development of the program. During this time Scharf joined the faculty at the University of California, Irvine, and his support was necessarily restricted to periodic visits. In 1974 Hickey helped establish the New Haven group home largely with the financial backing of the New Haven Foundation. Here, day-to-day responsibility rested with the local YWCA personnel who provided the facility.

The following year a national training center was established at Niantic under Hickey's direction, and, with financing by the National Institute of Corrections, the male unit described herein was opened. In all these endeavors numerous individuals in both the corrections department and Harvard University played vital roles. By 1977, the training center had developed seven democratic interventions around the country in addition to the two units at Niantic. Several high school programs also borrowed heavily from this work.

The present book got underway in the spring of 1976. As the work progressed, however, it became clear that our theoretical interests had dramatically shifted. We were no longer simply interested, for example, in inmate reform. Rather, our inquiring had shifted to a reexamination of the moral validity of the prison itself. The various constraints, whether legal or administrative, and their implications for both staff and inmate, began to occupy both our theoretical and practical discussions. Perhaps this shift is most graphically illustrated by the change in the project's name from "Moral Treatment Unit" in 1971 to the "Just Community Project" from 1975 onward. In any event, it became obvious by 1978 that a new direction in the correctional enterprise was needed. We also became convinced that the Just Community approach could help define that direction. Hickey joined the faculty at the University of New Haven in 1978, primarily to rethink the entire Just Community approach in light of the new ideas that emerged during the training center phase.

It is impossible for us to individually name the many people who played a significant role in the formation of this book. Certain people, however, should be mentioned. We wish to thank Commissioner John R. Manson, who not only supported our efforts, but from time to time kept the wolves away; Deputy Commissioner Janet York, whose practical skill and honesty kept us constantly raising impossible questions; Robert Brooks, director of program development of the corrections department in Connecticut, who was always available for help and encouragement; and former Commissioner Ellis MacDougall, who was the first to encourage our work. We also wish to publicly thank Craig Dobson and Michael Garrity of the National Institute of Corrections, as well as Richard Graham of Washington, D.C., for their encouragement and understanding.

If Estelle Brown, David Konefal, James Reis, Charles Hecksher, Peter Baumgartel, and Gary Gordon—our unit supervisors and trainers—were the project's heart and mind, then the line officers, particularly Ellen Thomas and Alice Perkins—who helped start the program and are still carrying it on—were its soul. We also wish to recognize the hundreds of inmates throughout the country and particularly at Niantic who shared the past ten years with us.

Special recognition is given to Lawrence Kohlberg of Harvard University; without his help and encouragement, there would have been no Just Community Project. We value him as both a colleague and a friend.

This work represents a joint effort and equal participation by the authors; we assume full responsibility for the content and opinions expressed herein.

January 1980   JOSEPH E. HICKEY
                                        Southington, Connecticut

                                            PETER L. SCHARF
                                        San Clemente, California

Contents

The Authors

JOSEPH E. HICKEY is associate professor of criminology, Division of Criminal Justice, at the University of New Haven. He was awarded the B.A. degree in philosophy from Saint Anselm's College (1963), the M.A. degree in special education from Central Connecticut State College (1968), and the Ed.D. degree in psychology and education from Boston University (1972).

    Hickey is the author of several articles on moral development, criminal justice, and prisons. His professional affiliations include the American Correctional Association, the National Council on Crime and Delinquency, and the National Academy of Criminal Justice Educators. He is presently working on another book dealing with the ethics of imprisonment.

PETER L. SCHARF is assistant professor of social ecology, Program in Social Ecology, at the University of California, Irvine. He was awarded the B.A. degree in history from the University of Rochester (1967), the master's in education from Harvard University (1970), and the Ed.D. in developmental psychology from Harvard University (1973).

    Scharf has published *Readings in Moral Development* (1978), *Growing Up Moral* (1979), and numerous articles on penology,

police science, and education. Currently he is serving as project
director of a large national study on the police use of violent force.

To Our Parents

Toward a Just Correctional System

Experiments in Implementing Democracy in Prisons

1

Democratic Process and the Criminal Justice System

One night one of us, while a consultant to a large state prison, observed an "inmate council" meeting, in which five denim-clad inmate representatives conferred with five well-dressed prison administrators. The latter were comfortably seated in leathered office furniture. The inmates sat on battered wooden chairs that they had brought with them from their cells. As the two sides talked about replacing light bulbs in the gym and putting more towels in the shower room, the consultant noticed a large tattoo on one inmate's arm reading *Born to lose!*

At first this message seemed proper, almost expected. Mass murderer Richard Speck had worn the same tattoo. After all, prisons are typically supposed to house the losers of society, the violent, the malicious, the stupid, although one might argue that it is the *non*-prisoners who are the losers, since it is society that pays up to $25,000 a year to finance each prisoner's incarceration, including the make-work and pseudotherapy. Yet, as one stared at the tattoo, it seemed to take on a larger meaning: Were not both prisoner and prison born to lose? And could nothing save either one?

The events in the inmate "council" seemed to confirm this sense of futility. The council, created some six months before to "further positive communications" between inmates and prison, had been prompted by a sit-down strike of Hispanic and black inmates who charged guard brutality, racism, and corruption. But when the newly formed council began addressing these and other serious issues it was summarily suspended by its founder, the warden, and one of the most vocal inmate representatives was transferred to another facility. Now, most other inmates neither participated in nor cared about the council—it spent its time debating towels and light bulbs, even though the prison *was*, in fact, overcrowded, the guards often brutal and racist, and the staff rife with corruption. Thus, while administrators pretended to listen and communicate, they ignored or denied the prisoners' desires, confirming what both knew—that both were born to lose.

Is there any *realistic* way it could be different? What are the chances of developing a program in which prisoners feel that they are "born to win"—not because of a psychological goal on the part of the administrators to "rehabilitate their self-concept" but rather because of a genuine belief that prisoners as persons deserve respect, kindness, and opportunity?

This notion is not entirely new. In this chapter, we describe three democratic prison reform movements that attempted to use the prison as a training ground in democratic values. These reforms and the reformers behind them are not without paradox and contradiction. Few of the reforms lasted more than five years, and none was able to achieve a permanent change in the manner in which inmates were treated or regarded. Thus, in describing the efforts of such reformers as Alexander Maconochie, Thomas Mott Osborne, and Elliot Studt, we not only analyze the social philosophy underlying their crusades but also critically assess the reasons for their demise.

The topic of democratic prison reform has in recent years stimulated little interest, although as late as the 1930s inmate self-government often was believed to be the most promising idea to those interested in penal reform. Edwin Sutherland, in his *Principles of Criminology* (1939), observed that inmate self-government was the most commonly proposed solution to prison discipline and reform. As early as 1793, for instance, a modified form of prison self-government was used in Philadelphia's Walnut Street Jail. In the nineteenth and the early twentieth centuries, Maconochie ([1839] 1967), Hatch ([1885] see Helfman, 1950), George (1910), Brockaway (1912), Osborne (1916), and Gill (1937), among others, implemented and maintained, even if only for short periods, seemingly viable prison democracies. These efforts at democratic prison reform have been justified by one or more of the following rationales—*educational, environmental, legal,* and *moral.* We discuss each in turn.

Educational Rationales

Thomas M. Osborne, whose Mutual Welfare League is discussed in greater length in this chapter, offered a civic education rationale for the democratization of prison life. His ideology contained elements of both a Jeffersonian democratic faith in human potential and a Deweyite belief that democratic experience begets democratic attitudes. In *Society and Prisons* (1916, p. 154), Osborne declared, "Outside the walls, a man must choose between work and idleness. . . . (Why not let himself teach these lessons before he goes out?). . . . Such things are best taught by experience. So inside your walls you must have courts and laws to protect those who are working from the idle thief. And we must rest assured that the laws would be made and the laws enforced. The prison must be an institution where every inmate must have the largest possible freedom, because it is liberty that fits men for liberty."

Osborne, a supporter of George's Junior Republic movement, cited earlier, was probably also influenced by the work of social philosophers Charles Cooley and George Herbert Mead. Democracy, they theorized, required democratic thinkers, and only by experimenting with self-government could one learn to respect the underlying social principles implicit in the American constitution. In *Prisons and Common Sense* (1924, pp. 41–42), Osborne used Cooley's notion of learning through experimental role playing to justify giving inmates experience in democratic life:

In some prison schools will be found a class in civics.
That is very well—all knowledge is useful; but it has little
relation to real training in citizenship. As every boy knows,
the only way to learn to play baseball is to play it. An attempt
to make pitchers, catchers, batters, and baserunners by studying the rules and reading a history of the game would be so
ridiculous that even penologists have not suggested it; even in
prisons where it is permitted, they actually play ball instead of
studying. So with citizenship: To know how to be a good
citizen—to do one's duty to the community and encourage
one's fellow citizens to do theirs; to claim one's own rights
without infringing upon the rights of others; to learn by one's
mistakes; to trust and not be discouraged when deceived; to be
trusted and stand up under it—to learn how to do even a part
of these and other necessary things, a man must actually do
them. Fortunately, it is not impossible—even in prison.

Osborne's work influenced a large number of prison reformers
of the post-World War I generation. For example, Lane (1919, p. 173),
an early twentieth-century advocate of democratic prison reform,
suggested, "Self-government in penal institutions is simply an application of the educational principle that people learn by doing. Its
method is to establish on a small scale a society in which [the inmate]
. . . can form habits that make normal life attainable. By its very
operation, self-government identifies each inmate with his fellow
inmates." For Osborne and his followers, democratic prison reform
was essentially an educational tool. Rejecting the congregate work
theory of the late nineteenth and early twentieth centuries, which
required prisoners to collectively toil in silence for long hours without compensation, they sought through democratic experiences to
teach democratic values and ideals to simultaneously change the
inmate's respect for the prison and for the larger social order.

Environmental Rationales

A second group of reformers has focused more on the positive
impact self-government can have on the quality of the prison environment than on the educational benefits it may produce. A 1958 study by
Gresham M. Sykes of a New Jersey prison recognizes that the very
nature of traditional prisons requires a certain amount of illicit self-

government. Given the prison's totalitarian structure, the prisoner lacks any legitimate grounds for cooperation with his or her captors. Thus when his or her cooperation is required for such things as the operation of prison industries the captor must tacitly buy the cooperation of key inmate "elites," who in turn coerce cooperation and order among weaker prisoners. Sykes notes (1958, p. 128), "This illicit form of inmate self-government contains . . . the seeds for . . . particularly brutal assault of one inmate on another which can be traced to a quarrel over the distribution of contraband. A disgruntled guard, irritated by the power of the inmate 'big shots,' may catch the attention of the newspapers, as may a discharged prisoner anxious to settle an old grudge."

Clearly, self-government of this type makes a mockery of the democratic ideals that prisons are supposed to uphold. Yet the reality of inmate power must somehow be reckoned with. Charles and Gabrielle Stastny (1977) have argued that in the Washington state prison they studied democratic participation provided (at least for a short time) a mechanism for resolving conflict among contending inmate groups as well as between the prison administration and the prisoners.

Interestingly enough, this political defense of democracy has been advocated by both conservative and radical penologists. Conservatives, such as Gill (1931) and Baker (1973a, 1973b), see prison democracy as an effective means of pacifying or channeling inmate discontent. When we interviewed a contemporary eastern sheriff (John Buckley) who has started a successful prison advisory system, he observed that the inmate council had replaced both the "stoolie" and the "dogs" (inmate leaders) as a means of control. Radicals such as Irwin (1973), Mathiesen (1974), and Huff (1974) see democratic participation as a useful tool for negotiating prison conflict provided that there exists an inmate union, external advocacy group, or other effective means of enforcing inmate interests. They tend to view prison democracy as a political means of raising inmate consciousness and attracting outside attention to the plight of prisoners. Huff observes that inmate unionization may evolve from a concern with the problems of specific prisoners to a concern with the larger political issues implied in the very existence of prisons. As evidence, he offers the following statements by KRUM, the Swedish prisoners' union in 1967 and 1971, respectively:

> [KRUM] will attend to the interests of those who are punished, and ease their readjustment to society. KRUM works for a radical *reform* of the correctional system and the *treatment* of prisoners. Legislation and treatment of criminals ought to be liberated from punitive thinking. The present system of institutions ought to be abolished, and incarceration reduced to a minimum. Offenders who have social handicaps ought to be met by a social policy which is liberated from moralizations and authoritarian thinking.
>
> [KRUM] wishes to analyze and fight the *class society*, which through its unequal distribution of power and opportunity contributes to the creation of groups which are socially, economically, and culturally expelled.

As Huff (1974, p. 8) writes, "KRUM is working to abolish imprisonment and other types of forced incarceration within the correctional system, child and youth welfare, mental health care, alcohol care, narcotics care, handicap care, and so on."

Legal Rationales

There are several established inmate legal rights in the areas of civil liberties, due process, and judicial review, but in actuality few of these rights can be claimed. For example, although inmates accused of a disciplinary offense are guaranteed administrative due process rights, in practice these rights are often denied or manipulated by disciplinary boards manned exclusively by prison staff. Prison democracy has been seen as a means of preserving these rights, which are supposedly guaranteed by the U.S. Constitution. Boards or juries made up of both inmates and staff might ensure a greater chance of fairness than would all-inmate or all-staff boards. Similarly, the right to bring witnesses and to cross-examine them would probably be better assured under a democratic framework than under one imposed solely by the prison administration. In contrast to the notion of prison democracy, Goldfarb and Singer (1973) suggest that inmate rights can be protected only by establishing some form of regular inspection by an ombudsman or by developing inmate collective bargaining. Fogel (1973) has also argued that arbitration or ombudsman schemes provide the best means toward achieving prison justice.

Despite the arbitration and ombudsman suggestions, it has been plausibly argued, both in general political theory as well as penology, that democratic participation is a better means of assuring just treatment of legal claims, by both majority and minority, than is justice imposed by even well-meaning prison administrators. In democratic systems, with adequate checks and balances and with appellate review, there are protections against a "tyranny of the majority" over minority rights. This argument assumes that prison inmates have both the will and ability to impartially arbitrate social conflict and to administer justice to other inmates, with at least as much skill as the average warden or discipline board.

Moral Rationale

One early articulate advocate of democratic reform as a means of attaining justice was Alexander Maconochie, whose nineteenth-century contributions will be discussed shortly. Commenting on the traditional ways prison administrators dealt with prisoners, he wrote, "We habitually make a number of mistakes . . . to which all disciplinarians are zealously attached. We draw no distinction between moral and conventional offenses. By minute regulation, we multiply the number of the latter and exaggerate their importance. . . . We sear their consciences . . . with petty offenses. We allow the higher principles of human nature to lie dormant in our prisoners. We make no appeal but immediate submission" ([1839] 1967, p. 32). Maconochie believed that the ultimate justification for democratic prison reform was the human worth of the prisoners themselves.

Types of Prison Democracies

J. Baker, in his *Right to Participate* (1973b), counts nearly a hundred examples of American democratic prison reforms, ranging from "symbolic" honor councils to programs allowing inmates a voice in the conduct of prison life. Table 1 distinguishes two dimensions of prison democracy: (1) *range* of influence of inmate participation (influence on only a living or work group versus prison-wide influence) and (2) *mode* of power (representative, or direct). We will discuss these in turn and then indicate the types of issues allocated to each.

Table 1. Types of Participation.

	Range of Influence (Model)	
Mode of power	Decentralized	Centralized
Representative	Type 1 (Unit representative council)	Type 2 (Prison representative council)
Direct	Type 3 (Unit direct democracy)	Type 4 (Prison direct democracy)

Range of Influence and Mode of Power. Decentralized participation and centralized participation differ in range of influence. Decentralized government bodies affect small living or work groups. The prison auto shop supervisor who creates a shop democracy influences only the members of the shop while they are assigned to that activity. Centralized participation, however, affects the prison as a whole.

Participation differs also in the mode of power exerted. Representative power is that power legitimately delegated to representatives of a larger constituency. Direct power requires active participation by all inmates in prison decision making. What follows are decentralized small group and centralized large-scale examples of these modes of power. An example of decentralized representative power is the cottage or shop advisory group (Type 1). Often inmates are appointed by officials rather than elected. Usually they meet weekly to advise the staff about inmate views. In one Colorado prison, for instance, the "dorm advisory board" served mostly to provide orientation for new inmates. In times of crisis, an advisory board may be used to pacify or to negotiate with key inmates. Often the representative or advisory system has little power and mostly exerts symbolic influence.

The centralized prison representation council (Type 2) is the most common form of inmate participation (Murton, 1974). Here inmate representatives meet with the warden to express their views.

For example, in the Massachusetts Middlesex House of Correction, according to Sheriff John Buckley (personal communication, 1976) inmates' representatives meet weekly with a staff board to review rules and policies. Issues might range from a pizza night proposal to more fundamental changes in guard-inmate relationships. Members of a council are often appointed by staff or administration. Sometimes, however, they are elected at large. Generally, they have neither the power to discipline nor the power to allocate resources.

Decentralized direct democracy (Type 3) requires participation in a community meeting format. It is usually most effective in a living unit rather than in a work unit. Both inmates and staff can raise issues of concern, and community rules must be binding on both.

Centralized direct democracies (Type 4) are rare. There have been unusual situations, such as during recent guard strikes in Connecticut and New York state, in which inmates exercised a great deal of "legitimate" direct power through democratic process for several days, or the 1971 Attica insurrection, which quickly developed an ad hoc committee, a representative system, that made most of the major decisions during the week-long protest (Wicker, 1974).

While each of these types defines "participation" in prisons, only small group (decentralized) direct participation and large-scale (centralized) representative models have enough historical examples and enough evidence of effect on both prison and inmates to be labeled genuine democratic participation. "Honor boards" or "advisory councils," both small unit and large group, only rarely have any prolonged effect on either prison policies or other inmates. Unit representative councils tend to involve so few inmates as to be of negligible importance.

Type of Issues Allocated. Prison democracies may be differentiated by types of issues allocated. Some programs allow inmates to deal with only minor housekeeping or recreation rules; for example, which television programs are to be watched or who should clean which tier. Other programs allow inmate participation in minor disciplinary offenses—for example, offenses not involving serious use of contraband or confrontation with an officer. Few programs allow inmates to participate in major discipline decisions; for example, those involving escape, bodily harm, or conflicts with an officer. None allow inmates to have input into major policy decisions; for example, whether or not to build a new prison or hire new staff. Although these extensions of inmate power historically have been rare, they are essential to any program that, in Murton's phrase (1974), moves beyond a "token" effort at democratization.

Maconochie's Norfolk Island Experiment

On March 6, 1840, Captain Alexander Maconochie, formerly of the British Royal Navy, was appointed to serve as superintendent of an Australian penal colony located on Norfolk Island some 900 miles east-north-east of Sydney. His appointment was occasioned by a series of recommendations he had made in a report of penal conditions on the island of Van Dieman's (now Tasmania) a few years before. The British authorities were sufficiently impressed with his "mark system" concept that he was requested to implement it. Clearly, Norfolk Island was not the ideal site for an untested penal theory. For years, it had served as the dumping ground for those called "irreclaimables" from the other penal colonies. Indeed, conditions were so dreadful at Norfolk that a Catholic priest who visited in 1834 to minister to a group of condemned men reported that the few who received last-minute reprieves wept with sorrow at the prospect of living, while the doomed fell to their knees in thanksgiving.

Briefly, Maconochie's mark system, which he refined during his four years as superintendent of Norfolk, rests as much on his personal moral outrage at the cruelties he had observed in the British penal system as on his recognition that, as a practical matter, his prisoners were economically vital in a sparsely populated untamed region. Thus, instead of time sentencing, he instituted labor sentencing, by which the prisoners earned their freedom. Operationally, the convict earned a predetermined number of "marks" as a condition of his release, the total number being determined by the nature of the offense. A fair day's work was fixed at 10 marks. To assure that the men worked efficiently, they were paid by the piecework system. For every 10 marks earned, the convict shortened his imprisonment by a day. The marks were also used for commissary purchases, including food, as well as for disciplinary purposes. In this way, the prisoner was placed in control of his sentence and provided with numerous opportunities to regulate the quality of his life-style.

Besides the mark system, Maconochie restructured the sentences into four phases. The first, the penal stage, required the men to work under rigorous discipline. The second, social, stage provided them with an opportunity to form their own work companies of about six men. Here their marks were pooled in common. Food and fines were deducted from the pool. Maconochie particularly encouraged inmate self-government within this structure. In the third (individualized) stage, the groups were dissolved, and each man was encouraged to maintain a small bit of property as he saw fit. Most of the men apparently planted small gardens and maintained livestock, which they kept or traded. The only major requirement was that they continue their piecework labor until they earned their "ticket of leave" and passed to the fourth stage, which permitted them freedom for the balance of their sentence, provided they committed no further offenses.

Many of Maconochie's initial reforms appear to be more derived from common sense rather than from a formal penal philosophy. For example, he insisted that the "mess" have knives, forks, and a few cooking utensils. Underlying such efforts was his conception that prisoners had the right to personal dignity. He also saw that the old system discouraged any prisoner initiative. He saw that some of them, in fact, were more trustworthy and moral than those guarding them. It would appear that Maconochie's reasoning for establishing self-governing work teams (Phase 2) foreshadowed contemporary sociological thinking concerning socialization processes. He writes ([1839] 1967, p. 24), "That to strengthen these moral checks and stimulants, when prisoners are kept together in numbers they may be distributed into small parties (say) of six, with common interests. Each man is thus laboring for others, as well as for himself. By this means, it is hoped to implant and cultivate kindly and social feelings, instead of the intensely selfish ones which usually characterize the criminal, and especially grow up in the solitude of an unconnected crowd."

After four extremely successful years of operation, the local governor withdrew his support of Maconochie and his experiment. This seems to have been precipitated by two issues. First, the mark system, based as it was on the individual's labor, was at odds with a time sentence policy demanded by the English Parliament as necessary for both individual and collective deterrence. Second, there was strong opposition to the transportation system in general, particularly among Australians who were forced to accept the released men. Because Maconochie's system worked, in the sense that significant numbers of prisoners survived their sentences, political pressure was exerted to put an end to it. A face-saving excuse was conveniently provided by Maconochie himself. He had permitted his inmates to have what amounted to one dram of whiskey per person, diluted in a fruit punch, in honor of Queen Victoria's birthday. When the story was circulated, the governor had ample reason to demand Maconochie's removal.

Back home, Maconochie defended his efforts by comparing the moral assumptions underlying the mark system with those underlying the Benthamite notion of utilitarian deterrence, on which rested the British system of fixed-time sentencing. The mark system, he said, required the maintenance of the dignity of the inmate as a moral end in itself, whereas the utilitarian system required maintenance of inmate dignity only insofar as it was a means to securing the welfare of the society as a whole. If deterrences required the total degradation of the offender, this was, in Bentham's phrase, a "moral good."

Did Maconochie's system actually work? Sir George Gipp, governor of New South Wales and therefore Maconochie's supervisor, visited the penal colony unexpectedly in 1843 and found "good order everywhere to prevail, and the demeanor of prisoners to be respectful and quiet" (Barry, 1958). Maconochie himself claimed that he maintained perfect order and tranquility; that he found the island "a turbulent, brutal hell and left it a peaceful, well-ordered community." Eyewitness testimony by a local churchman who ministered to the prisoners supports that Maconochie succeeded beyond all reasonable expectations. Did his system work with respect to recidivism? Approximately 1,450 prisoners were discharged during Maconochie's superintendency. The percentage of reconvictions was less than 3 percent. Barry (1958) reports that of the 920 supposedly "irreclaimables" released only 20 were known to be reconvicted. Unfortunately the available data is sketchy. Yet one thing seems certain: Prison order and the quality of life for the prisoners were vastly improved under Maconochie's system. Indeed, he succeeded in treating his prisoners as ends in themselves.

Perhaps the great irony in the Maconochie saga, however, is the fact that he did indeed provide a major impetus for subsequent penal practice in ways he never anticipated. His arguments in behalf of inmate reform as against deterrence gradually gained acceptance. Fixed sentencing finally gave way to indeterminate sentences and the consequent development of probation and parole. The essence of his mark system, however—the self-determinate sentence—has never been fully appreciated. Thus, his great genius in deriving a sentencing structure that recognized human worth, permitted control over one's destiny, and encouraged personal responsibility has been largely ignored or misunderstood. Indeed, it is likely that Maconochie, viewing modern penal practice, would be outraged at what was made of his efforts.

Osborne's Mutual Welfare League

More than seventy years after Maconochie's arrival on Norfolk Island, another effort was made to use democratic method and ideology to transform a major prison. In 1913, Thomas Mott Osborne, a wealthy businessman and former Democratic mayor of Auburn, New York, was appointed by a liberal New York governor to chair a state commission on prison reform. A Harvard graduate and Wilsonian liberal, Osborne had been long concerned about the nation's prisons. Unlike many reformers pontificating about prison horrors from behind comfortable desks, Osborne knew he was ignorant of prison life and so arranged to be incarcerated for a week in intimidating Auburn Prison in order to personally observe the conditions. Although he adopted the alias Tom Brown, the inmates had been informed of his true identity by the warden.

His diary, published in 1916, reveals much about both the man and the conditions he encountered: "I am a prisoner, locked, double-locked. . . . I am a voluntary prisoner, it is true; nevertheless, even a voluntary prisoner cannot unlock the door of his prison cell. I am perfectly conscious of a horrible feeling of constraint—of confinement. . . . For me there is plenty to do—to write, to read, to think about—but how about those who do not care for reading . . . or cannot read or write? . . . The loneliness in the midst of invisible human beings, not one you can ever hear is quite indescribable; it can only be felt. . . . Inside my cell the electric bulb gives barely enough light to read by. . . . It is horribly lonesome" (Osborne, 1916, pp. 123, 127, 128).

During his week in prison, Osborne decided to see what the "cooler" (or segregation wing) was like and, refusing to work one day, was promptly removed to it. He writes, "It is admirably situated for performing the operation of breaking a man's spirit. For it has on one side the death chamber, and on the other the prison dynamo. . . . When Warden Rattigan came, the inmates slept on bare iron . . . formally the supply of water was limited to one gill [½ pint] for twenty-four hours. The sink was not used for the prisoners to wash, as the prisoners of the jail (cooler) were not allowed to wash . . . the aching, overwhelming sense of hideous cruelty of the whole barbaric business sweeps over me . . . of madness and suicide haunting the place" (Osborne, 1916, pp. 134–135).

Osborne largely credits the origin of the Mutual Welfare League to his work mate, Jack Murphy, and recorded what he later considered the germinal conversation with Murphy: "'Well, look here, Tom.' In his eagerness, Jack comes around to my side of the working table. 'I know this place through and through . . . I know these men . . . the big majority of them will be square with you if you give 'em a chance. . . . That's it, Tom, a good conduct league. Give the privileges of Sunday to the members of the league. Last year we got up an antiswearing league here in this shop, and we had a penalty for every oath. . . . The forfeits were paid in matches. . . . The Good Conduct League would be a much better thing. It would be just great. And go! Sure it'll go'" (Osborne, 1916, pp. 155–157).

In the autumn of 1913, Osborne proposed that all internal disciplinary offenses in Auburn Prison be turned over to a committee of forty-nine prisoner representatives, one from each of the work-shops. These men would form an inmate court as well as rotating grievance committee. At first, inmates balked against punishing "their own." After much debate, however, the prisoners voted to enforce their own discipline with the exception of assault on an officer, deadly assault on another inmate, refusal to work, strike, and attempted escape. The men agreed.

The representatives soon developed a constitution and called their organization the Mutual Welfare League. The league lasted twelve months, and under its auspices near-miracles occurred. Fights became rare. Injuries decreased. Assaults on guards became almost nonexistent. Escapes became rare. Work production increased.

The next year, the experiment was moved to Sing Sing Prison. Osborne relinquished his role as chairman of the prison reform commission to become warden of this larger and more difficult institution.

At Sing Sing, guards were asked to change their roles from that of hostile warders to something akin to that of modern counselor—correctional officer, what Osborne called "friends trying to help these men try to take their proper places in society." The result, as Osborne noted, was that "while the system has freed the prisoners, it has also freed the guards." One senior guard observed that "The men are putting forth their best endeavors to make the new movement a success. I also wish to say that during my sixteen years' experience, both in Elmira Reformatory and at Auburn Prison, it has never been so pleasant for me as it is now" (Tannenbaum, 1933, p. 95).

A whole range of recreational activities was introduced into the prison, including singing and playing in a prison band. Night school classes were also started, and one prisoner indicated the extent of inmate participation: "A Spanish class in which thirty-five men are enrolled. Following the lines laid down by Cortina, who donated fifty copies of *Spanish in 20 Lessons*, we have procured a native Spaniard for this class with surprisingly beneficial results. Attendance 90 percent.

"A class in mathematics with thirty pupils. This class was organized for a threefold purpose. First, as a base for the commercial class; second, as a base for the electrical class; and thirdly, as a means toward mental discipline, systematically teaching the men to think constructively. This class meets three times a week. A two-hour session is set aside for English composition. Attendance 100 percent!"

Attendance at a stenography class was 95 percent and was 100 percent at classes in mechanical drawing and telegraphy.

The structure of the Mutual Welfare League was as follows: A board of forty-nine delegates was elected by the prisoners for a term of six months. This body constituted a congress of delegates with various committee activities and legislative power. In times of serious disagreement, however, a general community meeting could be called to either support or counteract the actions of the delegates. The delegates elected an executive board of nine inmates, who in turn elected a sergeant at arms, a sort of police chief.

The executive committee handled most routine decisions, such as special shoes for the foundry workers or money for a guard's sick relative. The committee also handled conflicts between inmates and staff. When workers in the shoe shop appeared to be malingering, for example, an order to return to work was delivered by the executive committee on receiving a complaint (judged legitimate) by the captain.

An inmate court, consisting of five inmate judges serving terms of five months each, was responsible for most disciplinary infractions. The hearings were open to all members of the league. Appeals could be made to the warden's court composed of Osborne, the principal keeper, and the doctor, at which time the inmate judges were forced to defend the justice of their decision. Often more than a hundred inmates attended an appeals hearing.

In his biography, *Osborne of Sing Sing*, Tannenbaum (1933, pp. 162–163) suggests that such appeals served many useful purposes.

> Appeal gave the culprit a sense he had a fair trial. It compelled the judges to defend their decision in public before the warden and before the community on grounds that would appeal (seem fair) to both; the interests of the warden and the prison community thus united against the lawbreaker. It gave the warden an opportunity to know what was going on and an opportunity to lay down fundamental rules of policy which should govern not only the action of the prisoners but of the law-enforcing machinery. And it compelled the warden to behave in a manner that the prison community would recognize as just and fair. More important than that, it removed the warden from being the direct source of discipline and turned the sense of grievance against the court and the inmates' police, instead of focusing it on the warden. The importance of this can hardly be overemphasized. The warden stepped in between the irate community and its victim and pleaded for justice to the culprit. The warden could thus act in public as the friend and defender of the aggrieved. It automatically changed the position of the warden in relation to the problem of discipline. It made his authority no less. It made it more pervading, but changed the plane of his behav-

ior from a secret, arbitrary, and personal infliction of punishment to one of a public defense of the broad interest of the community at large. The warden per se thus came to stand for justice in the best sense of the word. The character of the inmate court at Sing Sing is indicated by the fact that the guards who at first demurred to testify before a group of prisoners and be examined by them, soon learned to defer to the judgment of the prisoners' court and to treat its members with deference and respect. That was a great moral victory for all concerned and was an unusual bit of evidence of the very real force for good discipline that these courts represented.

The Mutual Welfare League dealt with a broad range of inmate offenses and conflicts. One typical "docket" included fighting, refusal to work, insulting an officer, spitting in chapel, insulting the league, threatening delegates, gambling, using a weapon in a fight, smoking in line after bugle call, sodomy, and smoking in work.

Tannenbaum (1933, p. 166) describes a case that seems characteristic of those judged by the Sing Sing court:

> An Italian prisoner is brought to the bar by the warden's office and the Brotherhood's sergeant at arms, the case has already been prepared. The judges, with a preliminary knowledge of the facts, examine the culprit. It appears that he refused to obey the morning summons of his keeper to leave his cell for work in his shop. Evidence shows that, owing to some slip in the machinery, he was practically without shoes; also that the keeper more or less approved of the prisoner's action as a means of attracting attention to his needs. Although his prosecution is not vigorously pressed, the man receives from the court a disciplinary, though sympathetic, verdict. And in a minority opinion one of the judges reprimands him for breaking the prison's fundamental law—obedience, whatever the circumstances and however condoned by authority.

Conviction by the inmate jury typically meant suspension of an inmate's citizenship in the Mutual Welfare League for a specified period. This was usually sufficient to deter wrong action in that it returned the offender to his condition before the league went into effect; that is, into a system of unilaterally imposed prison discipline.

More stringent punishment included permanent banishment to a "nonleague" prison confinement.

The league was not without its contradictions. For one thing, it represented a privileged form of participation, ultimately dependent on the warden rather than a legally claimable right. While Osborne believed it was fatal to countermand any specific league decision ("The minute that the administration plays politics, trouble begins"), he was willing to make continuance of the league conditional on the inmates' maintenance of good order. On at least two occasions, he temporarily suspended the league's operation, removed its leadership, and the next day constituted a new league. Interestingly, the warden's right to temporarily abrogate the league's powers was carefully defined in the league's constitution.

Not all of the Sing Sing community was pleased with the Mutual Welfare League. There were a few inmates who by any criteria could not participate in such an idealistic enterprise. Also, the league council came to be dominated by a few inmate interest groups to the exclusion or possibly victimization of others. The "high-brow" (white-collar) inmates seem to have been hostile to the league both at Auburn and Sing Sing from its inception, and they often sought transfer to faraway rural prisons. This stemmed from the power of the "low-brow" inmates who, owing to their superior numbers, came to dominate the important league offices.

The policing of drugs and homosexuality also proved difficult. By turning such cases over to an inmate court, Osborne challenged the mores of the times, which prevented any rational discussion of these matters. Soon after the Mutual Welfare League began at Sing Sing, the conservative press attacked the right granted by Osborne for "convicted felons, rapists, drug-diseased maniacs, and other venomous fellows to judge their peers." They also condemned the existence of vice and sodomy, along with the "coddling of prisoners."

Despite its obvious accomplishments, the Sing Sing League lasted less than two years. Osborne's resignation illustrates some of the difficulties facing democratic prison reform. In 1916, the league handled a rather routine case of homosexuality. Afterwards, a local prosecutor, quietly aided by a hard-line law-and-order governor, obtained an indictment against Osborne on a number of charges, including that of his having "known and covered up public immorality among the inmates." Witnesses called by the prosecutor tended to be white-collar inmates threatened by the rise to power of lower-class inmates. Although the charges were clearly trumped up and Osborne never was convicted, in October 1916 he was forced to resign.

During the next few years, subsequent wardens attempted unsuccessfully to maintain the league's structure. The powers granted particularly to the inmate court, however, were gradually removed under the press of public and political pressure. By 1922, it had been stripped of most of its important functions. Less than six years after its inception, the great experiment was dead.

Studt's C Unit

Elliot Studt, a social worker and researcher at the University of California, Berkeley, assumed the primary problem with offenders to be moral, in the sense that they had demonstrated an inability to ascribe dignity, respect, and concern for others. She did not view this deficiency, however, as necessarily a personality weakness. Rather, the individual had failed, primarily through lack of opportunity, to develop adequate political and social competence. Her C Unit was to provide the context by which participants could experience numerous, often complex social interactions, which, she hypothesized, would provide opportunities for social skill building. For Studt, then, the C Unit community was viewed as an agent of inmate reform, not so much as a way to nurture individual intrapsychic growth, but rather as a means of developing political and social competency.

Accordingly, Studt attempted to create a "near-real world" environment within the unit through the interaction of various claims surrounding community issues. The dynamics of this problem-solving model included (Studt, 1968, p. 10):

1. Attention to problems of immediate concern to community members, as defined by inmates as well as by staff.
2. Collaboration of all persons relevant to the problem under consideration in the analysis of problems and in action to resolve problems.
3. Task-focused action involving commitment on the part of

all relevant persons, staff as well as inmates, to make the
changes indicated by problem analysis.
4. Evaluation of problem-solving success against standards
combining concern for the development of moral relationships with concern for the efficient manipulation of reality.

Studt's focus, however, was largely limited to the unit itself.
She, unlike Maconochie and Osborne, accepted the legitimacy of the
larger prison with its bureaucratic management and carefully defined
role for staff and inmates. Thus, the C Unit was completely dependent on it for all essentials, including food, shelter, discipline, recreation, and work. Given the limited nature of her intervention, then, it
is not surprising that self-government existed primarily in several ad
hoc committees and focused largely on issues pertaining to the personal comfort of the inmates such as recreational and housing
accommodations, while leaving such matters as admission procedures and discipline in the hands of the larger prison staff.

The action phase began in September 1960 with the transfer of
twenty inmates into an empty prison wing designated the C Unit. It
was located at the Deuel Vocational Institution (DVI), about sixty
miles east of San Francisco, near the town of Tracy, California. The
population was evenly distributed between inmates under the juris-
diction of the California Department of Corrections, which ran the
prison, and a younger sample from the California Youth Authority,
who were serving generally shorter sentences.

Because the goal was to encourage community within the unit
through problem solving, little structure was provided other than
scheduled community meetings. Lacking the traditional prison reg-
imen, long-standing problems such as racial tensions and hostility
between the two jurisdictional groups began asserting themselves.
Further, many of the prisoners were angry and frightened at having
been unilaterally reassigned to a unit they neither had requested nor
understood. Moreover, the population size was increasing almost
daily in order to bring the unit up to capacity at 135 inmates. As a
result, the community meetings quickly became noisy gripe sessions,
and both staff and residents began predicting that things were going
to "blow." Gradually, however, small ad hoc meetings evolved
around specific concerns and their success served to encourage further
problem-solving sessions.

By December, four functional groups had emerged (Studt, 1968, p. 73):

1. Community groups for staff and inmate communication about mutual concern.
2. Task groups to do specific jobs for the unit.
3. Counseling groups for discussion of personal problems of inmates.
4. Interest groups for inmates with common leisure-time interest.

By the end of its first year, the program evidenced clear signs of a successful, albeit limited, self-governing community. This was perhaps most dramatically demonstrated when during an institution-wide racial disturbance the unit remained calm and conducted business as usual. Accordingly, several proposals were made by Studt to the institution's management designed to increase opportunities for unit responsibility.

Studt describes the results as follows (1968, pp. 280–281):

> Three particular failures to achieve the desirable organizational conditions for a resocializing community seem to account in large part for C Unit's inability to stabilize the potentialities for community that emerged toward the end of the first program year.
>
> Of primary importance was the fact that the community was never permitted to design its institutions for control in congruence with the values espoused in its welfare institutions. Sentencing, the honor system, and the DVI discipline process all remained static throughout the project's life, reflecting a quite different model for relating staff and inmates from that proposed by the project. Under these circumstances, C Unit inmates gained tangible and visible rewards from the larger system only for conformity as individuals, not for active participation in building community. The sanctioning system imposed from outside the project was a powerful force maintaining the "do your own time" orientation among the C Unit inmates. The fact that nothing could be done to change the means for dealing with deviant behavior created strong pressures against open community discussion of this critical area. The community's inability to act except in procuring amenities ultimately led to a sub rosa

acknowledgment between staff and inmates that the C Unit community was an artifact, not a dynamic and effective social entity. "Shuck" and "front" superseded commitment and respect, and "community" and "problem solving" became the false verbal coinage of a realm in which one did not "talk serious" in public.

The lack of problem-solving connections between the project and upper-level administration in DVI was in large part responsible for turning the C Unit community into an ineffective satellite. For a period of time, problem solving appeared in C Unit as the dominant process in many social relationships. But the dynamics of change so released were quickly blocked when the project's controlling environment continued to make decisions that reflected a different philosophy of action. The administration of the larger institution could not be drawn into the problem-solving process within the project, nor was it able to support such a process between itself and the project administration. In consequence, the administration of the larger institution could neither understand nor respond positively to the project's requests for increased responsibility.

The co-optation of the C Unit community was completed when a project supervisor was appointed to reinstate within the project the style of administration characteristic of the larger institution.

The Reasons for Failure

While the C Unit project is a far less powerful example of self-government compared to Maconochie's mark system or Osborne's Mutual Welfare League, the difficulties faced by the three projects seem quite similar. In each case, the mandate of the prison democracy was soon infringed on.

Motivated by the realities of a system steeped in a tradition of absolute power maintenance, administrators eventually perceived the democratic experiment as threatening to their control of the larger prison system. While initially administrators saw the experiment as contributing to better control, its continued existence appeared to them to erode that control. Eventually, tensions within the democratic community itself were used to justify the termination of the experiment. In all three cases, political support of the project was first modified and later withdrawn, and the "reformer" progressively harassed and either dismissed or forced to resign.

Such an outcome is quite predictable from the perspective of sociological theory. In his *Political Parties* (1915), Michels long ago suggested that almost all organizations tend eventually to be dominated by small oligarchies that rule hierarchically. Even in groups committed to extreme versions of individual freedom and democracy (for instance, the French anarchist parties), the complexity of organizational task demands administrative specialists. This tendency Michels ([1915] 1978, p. 377) refers to as the "iron law of oligarchy."

In prisons, internal constraints against democracy are accentuated. Sutherland (1939) observed that prison democracies often become dominated by inmate elites who govern largely for their own economic and political interests. For example, Warden Lawes (1932), who came to Sing Sing Prison four years after the demise of Osborne, found that the Mutual Welfare League had degenerated into an inmate oligarchy. He wrote (1932, p. 138), "I found the league divided into two party camps. The energies of both parties were concentrated toward corraling votes. . . . As a result, the better element among the prisoners held themselves aloof from the league, and it became the plaything of the less desirable class of men. . . . The league officials had full charge of all visiting parties. There were gratuities, of course. . . . Also, the league had full charge and control of the store. Little supervision was given. . . . The judges were not always of the highest caliber. They [would] not examine facts with impartial personality."

Then, too, the prison power structure often militates against democratic participation by inmates. Prison guards often perceive inmate power as undermining their own (Sykes, 1958). It is interesting that the 1975 Tombs Prison guard strike in New York City was rooted in the guards' perception that prison authorities had acceded to political demands of the inmates. Sing Sing's guards apparently went along with Osborne's reforms but often without great enthusiasm. Similarly, administrators have often been opposed to efforts at inmate democratic participation; most wardens see prison democracy as a threat to their often near-unilateral power. Even treatment personnel have frequently voiced objections to increases in inmate political power, seeing it as conflicting with the implementation of psychological programs and services (Cressey, 1960).

Another serious obstacle for democratic reform lies in the conflict between public traditional law and institutional practice. This, we observed, was the direct cause of the fall of the Mutual Welfare League as well as of Maconochie's mark system. At Sing Sing, the prerogative of the reformer in such matters as trying cases of sodomy or petitioning for early release clearly conflicted with that of the public law. Many prison violations—homosexual sex, use of controlled substances, assault on other inmates—are felony offenses under the law, although few are tried as such. When an inmate-run court "tries" such matters, it may usurp powers proper to the courts. If the powers of the prison democracy are not carefully defined in terms of the larger correctional and legal systems, it threatens the prison democracy and places inmates in an untenable position. In addition, the fact that inmates have limited economic and legal rights (being able to strike, file suit, or at times even appeal for aid from the courts) means that the privileges granted by an experiment in prison democratization are highly tenuous.

Another difficulty is posed by the architectural design of most prisons. Marrero (1977, p. 38), for example, observes that

> The architecture and layout of most traditional prisons not only prevents the inmate from expressing his reactions but magnifies his perception of not having behavioral control. The employment of the cellblock observation system reinforces the inmate's feelings of subordination to staff and emphasizes his inability to influence the structure of his environment. He is continually aware that "unacceptable" behavior can bring a variety of punishments, including social isolation. He exists in an environment that is often overcrowded and overstructured, denying him the ability to meet personal needs. As a former convict so eloquently stated, "The prison system has become a means for physically and psychologically containing, controlling, and programming inmates. In the process, one's individuality, independence, sensitivity, and responsibility for self are systematically assaulted. It is a system that denies human expression and demands universal conformity and passive acceptance. A natural response . . . is to resist and undermine the system in every way possible." The traditional prison environment, with its emphasis upon control, conveys to the inmate that activities take place only to the extent that prison staff allow them. Staff can terminate

any activity at will by simply reordering the environment so
that its enactment is impossible. . . .

In order for democratic reform to be effective, inmates
must believe that their time, effort, and investment will gain
them tangible results. They have to believe that achieving
collective responsibility will make the environment responsive to their needs, thereby improving the quality of their
lives. It is hard to believe that the prison can be democratized
when inmates live in an environment in which they have no
real control and are subject to continual sources of apprehen-
sion and stress.

In addition, almost every effort to democratize prisons has
been damned by the media as the "coddling of criminals" or has been
accused of creating a "country club" environment for prisoners. The
public image of the inmate is that of a depraved, immoral individual.
The notion that inmates can act responsibly toward both the prison
staff and other inmates is hard for reformers to sell to the public.
Elected officials rarely advocate or mandate democratic prison
reform. At best, they tolerate its efforts, so long as the political risks of
doing so remain slight. At the sound of the first political alarm, the
reformers' friends soon become advocates of prison law and order,
dooming a nascent reform effort.

Is There Hope?

Interpretation of the failure of the democratic prison movement is influenced by political ideology, and liberal, radical, and
conservative critics have different opinions. For example, Murton
(1974) and Baker (1973a, 1973b) perceive the failures of the reform
movement as largely a result of a failure of will or obstruction by
particular administrators. These analyses emphasize internal political dynamics (for example, the warden's attitude) in determining the
longevity of the reform effort. In his *Inmate Participation in Prison
Management* (1974), Murton sees conspiracy behind nearly every
democratic reform failure. It is the "hostile politicians," in his view,
rather than the reformers who have doomed the democratic reform
movement. This view seems to us perhaps overly charitable toward
the courageous but often naive democratic reformers.

Several common failures may be attributed to Maconochie, Osborne, and Studt. These reformers, particularly Maconochie and Osborne, were rather romantic regarding the moral understanding of the inmates involved in their project. When reading their writings, one might perceive an image of the inmate as a hybrid of a Rousseauian noble savage and a well-meaning village Rotarian. Osborne refers to one Auburn road camp gang as "the most wonderful fellows I have ever met." Murton tends to romanticize inmates as "victims of circumstance" or "social casualties." Such a view ignores the reality stated by a contemporary of Osborne, Bowers (1920, p. 157), who visited the Sing Sing League and reported that "the vast majority of inmates do not care to even attempt self-government."

The romanticization of the inmates in the prison drama is paralleled by the stigmatization of the guards. Osborne, for example, seems much less convinced of his ability to rehabilitate the guards than the inmates. Symbolically, his efforts to give the inmates a field day at Auburn were undertaken at the expense of the guards. He was openly delighted when the guards were quarantined for a smallpox epidemic. He asserted it would "give them a sense of what imprisonment meant" and "allow protection" for his experiment. During Osborne's trial, several, but by no means most, of the guards testified against him. Osborne's supporters among the prison line staff seemed attracted to the "friendly" attitude of inmates rather than to a real commitment to the league's philosophy. There seems to have been little or no training of guards in the new approach and little involvement of the guards in the judicial mechanism of the league.

In contrast to the views of the liberals, radical theorists tend to explain the failure of democratic reform in terms of its ignoring the social class struggle underlying the efforts of reform. Thus, systemic variables are emphasized, as opposed to variables unique to particular settings or individuals. Goldsmith, for example, sees Osborne's as well as Murton's reform efforts as being disguised means to redirect inmate hostility and legitimate the power structure of the administration. She writes (Goldsmith, 1977, p. 58), "Tannenbaum (1933), in his allusion to the league's punitive judicial system, has pinpointed the basic flaw inherent in all the models described. . . . To attempt participatory democracy within the existing social control system of the prison is to basically affirm and legitimate the existing system of power arrangements. Most attempts at democratic decision making co-opt both the inmates and staff into becoming more committed to a punitive system. In the co-optation process, there is an insidious attempt on the part of the administration to deflect the anger of the inmates from the keepers to each other, since they are also responsible."

Finally, conservatives have criticized democratic prison reform as being impractical and have challenged the assumption that inmates have any moral or legal right to self-management at all. One warden, for example, writes as follows (Anonymous Prison Superintendent, 1977, p. 63):

> In a well-run institution, a variety of alternatives are, and should be, available to each prisoner. By this I don't mean the usual list of activities common in correctional facilities, but the major interrelated and coherent options, including physical betterment, academic growth, vocational skill acquisition, and especially personal planning for release and the future. For these options to be meaningful, the prison needs the freedom to choose or reject them. No available option should be socially impermissible, nor should the staff be excluded from the social influences that determine choices.
>
> The responsibility for providing sound choices, if one agrees that they should be provided, and for providing safety, openness, a tension-free atmosphere, and the intellectual climate that makes such choices truly free, falls on the staff. All responsibility falls on the staff. (Civilly, no untoward event or circumstance can be assigned to an inmate.)
>
> Over the generations, these obligations have been honored in the breach more than the observance, and the public has had every right to complain of mismanagement. Examples of mismanagement, however, do not justify no management at all as a viable alternative. To suggest that responsibility should, or even can, be vested in those who are legally excluded from the responsibility demonstrates, in my opinion, an incredible level of naivete.

Both conservative and radical criminologists share a profound pessimism; neither group believes that it is possible or desirable to share power with prisoners in prisons as they now exist. The radical believes the larger structure of the criminal justice system must be changed prior to any meaningful sharing with inmates. The conservative has little conviction that the democratic ideal is either applicable or needed within the context of the prison. In seeking to explain the failure of democratic reform, both radical and conservative penologists rightly focus on the external context of democratic reform. It is these constraints, they argue, that make active democratic participation at least unlikely, if not impossible.

In explaining failure by referring solely to the external context of the prison, however, such critics confuse difficulty with impossibility. Certainly, prison democracy faces overwhelming external constraints, but sharing power with prisoners need not necessarily fail. More importantly, such critics confuse practicality with what is really a matter of philosophy. That is, even if the effort to democratize prisons is considered difficult, this in itself says little about whether the commitments central to democracy should or should not be valued as valid goals.

Our own analysis of the century-long movement to democratize prisons gives us cause for cautious optimism. We grant that the impersonal environment of traditionally managed prisons prohibits self-government on a permanent basis. The success of Maconochie, Osborne, and Studt was largely the result of intangibles such as personal charisma, political power and the temporary needs of the bureaucracy faced with crisis. These reformers essentially acted as power brokers between the system and the inmates. They could offer democratic participation but not guarantee it. They could negotiate the privileges of democratic participation but not demand it as a legal right. In this role, the reformer is obviously extremely vulnerable and, given a shift in public sentiment or systemic needs, can be exiled. Still, we feel that democratic reform offers an ideological direction both consistent with the laws of American society and its underlying principles. We believe, however, that at least two essential elements were missing in all the past reform efforts—namely, an explicit psychological theory of democratic learning and a more adequate philosophy of punishment. In the next chapter, we outline a theory of democratic learning we believe is uniquely suited to experiments in democratic life as well as philosophically acceptable to those concerned with psychological manipulation in the name of prison therapy. We suggest that it offers a philosophical guide toward learning consistent with the values of a just and democratic society. We will discuss more on the philosophical aspects of punishment in Chapter Eight.

2

Applying Moral Development Theory to Corrections

Prison correction efforts make certain philosophical assumptions not only about human value but also about human psychology, and thus they determine how the inmate is defined as a person and the type of conditions he or she must endure. In this chapter, we examine the assumptions underlying the medical model and behavioral prison therapies, contrast them with a correctional approach derived from developmental theory, and show how their assumptions lead to radically different prison environments. We also suggest that, for purposes of prison reform, the philosophical assumptions underlying developmental theory have at least three advantages over those of the other theories. That is:

1. They are ideologically consistent with the ideals of a democratic society, which emphasize rational dialogue between fair-minded citizens.
2. They are concerned with changes in reasoning rather than changes brought about by insight into self or by behavior modification,

29

thus avoiding the narcissism of some forms of psychotherapy and the alleged "brainwashing" of some behavior modification.
3. The assumption of justice as the end of development is appropriate to prison reform in a pluralistic society committed to tolerance and respect for different beliefs.

The problem of what kind of psychological goals prisons should adopt is not, of course, just a recent concern. In the nineteenth century, for instance, penology was characterized by debate between two "schools." The Pennsylvania "silent" system advocated placing offenders in isolated cells to repent their sins. The Auburn (New York) congregate system advocated hard work performed in groups. Both systems are often authoritarian and brutal, and neither proved very effective. The silent system produced insanity as often as it did reform. The congregate system often produced little but lethargy, anger, and defeat. In the silent system, prison neglect was rationalized as creating a climate conducive to prayer. In the congregate system, overwork, poor recreation facilities, and staff brutality were justified as instilling the virtues of industry and hard work.

In the twentieth century, there has been a similar debate between neo-Freudian psychotherapy, which assumes that most delinquent behavior is caused by neurosis, and behavior modification, which holds that it is learned through mechanisms similar to normal social behavior. The neo-Freudians argue that the offender suffers from a personality disorder that should be treated, the way any other medical infirmity is. Slavson (1961) and Friedlander (1960), for instance, suggest that institutional treatment should be provided by psychologically trained personnel to help offenders gain insight into the causes of their delinquency. Behavioral learning theorists such as Bandura (1969), however, rather than defining criminals as "sick," hold that they have been rewarded by peers and possibly parents and teachers for the wrong type of social behaviors—for stealing cars, for example, rather than holding a job. The behavioral strategy, then, focuses on teaching socially acceptable behaviors. Let us consider an example of each ideology we have observed translated into prison practice.

An Example of a Psychotherapeutic Prison: O. H. Close School

Since the 1930s, there have been many efforts to use persons trained in psychotherapy in prisons. From 1969 to 1972, for example, the O. H. Close training school in Stockton, California, under the auspices of the California Youth Authority, implemented a rather sophisticated program in which the entire staff was trained in the techniques of Transactional Analysis, a form of psychotherapy pioneered by the late Eric Berne, author of *Games People Play* (1964) and other books. Guards, cooks, and social workers were taught Berne's three ego states—the Child or the playful self ("I wanna have fun"), the Parent or restrictive and denying self ("You better not"), and the Adult or rational self ("Better not, because in the long run it's better to keep my job"). In addition, they received intensive training in "games" (crossed transactions), "life script" analysis (recognition of maladaptive interpersonal style), and basic therapeutic procedures.

State wards entering the prison were asked to formulate a series of written agreements called "contracts" with both counselors and institution. These contracts might specifically relate to personal style ("I will not get depressed"), social behavior ("I will not take advantage of weaker wards"), or academic performance ("I will bring my reading up to grade level"). For example (from authors' taped observations):

Ward: You can remind me of my goal every time you see me start to lose my cool.

Counselor: I'll do that. And there is something more you can do for yourself. When you start to lose your temper, or if you lose it once in a while, you can refuse to hassle yourself and use it as something to learn by. In that way, you can stop feeling badly about yourself.

Ward: I want to stop getting in fights.

Counselor: How are you going to do that?

Ward: By recognizing that I am in my old bag every time I feel myself ready to fight . . .

Counselor: Good. What can I do?

Counselors made an obvious effort to treat the wards with friendly respect, and wards were allowed to feel free to analyze "games" played by their counselors. Wards generally perceived their counselors as being helpers in a process of change. Rewards such as passes, privileges, and recreation opportunities were distributed in accordance with the staff's perception of a ward's progress.

A ward's release from the prison depended in part on his understanding the cause of his delinquency. As one inmate told us, "They let you out of here when you understand your problems . . . like about how my Child takes over when I get loaded. . . . Now, when my Child starts coming up, I use my Adult."

An Example of a Behavioral Prison: Karl Holton School

Another prison we observed, the Karl Holton School, also in Stockton, California, operated through a complex system of behavioral rewards, quite different from the psychotherapy prison. Wards were informed on arrival that they would leave the prison when they had acquired 7,875 points. By demonstrating "acceptable" behavior— that is, performing well in school and work—and by extinguishing "critical behavior deficiencies," the inmate was rewarded by receiving Behavioral Change Units (BCU's). Every day, an inmate was observed by staff, and for each positive behavior he was given a specified number of BCU's—for example, five for being on time to school, ten for neatly making his bed, five for controlling an angry temper all day, fifteen for passing a math test. Similarly, an inmate might lose BCU's—ten for making a messy bed, fifteen for failing a spelling test, and up to 3,000 for a fight. BCU's translated into "release" credits and into credits known colloquially as "funny money" that could be used to purchase from a "menu" of institutional privileges, or what a behavioral psychologist would call "immediate reinforcements" (see Table 2). As in O. H. Close, inmates formed contracts that determined a ward's therapeutic goals and the types of behaviors that would be rewarded or extinguished.

The Moral Disadvantages of Psychotherapeutic
and Behavioral Approaches

We do not concern ourselves here with the usual critique of treatment approaches. Martinson (1974) has recently reviewed var-

Table 2. Holton School Reinforcement "Menu" of Institutional Privileges That Could Be Purchased with BCU's ("Funny Money").

	BCU's		BCU's
1. Canteen (fee)	$ 10	18. Packages, personal	$ 25
2. Change of bed area	300	19. Clothing, personal (per	
3. Consultation (other than		item)	10
hall staff)	20	20. Radio, personal	75
4. Day pass, regular	100	21. Record player, personal	200
5. Day pass, extended	150	22. Ping-Pong, ½ hour	15
6. Furlough	1000	23. Ping-Pong ball	5
7. Grooming aid (per item)	5	24. Pool table, ½ hour	35
8. Ice call	20	25. Popcorn popper	10
9. Iron, use of	10	26. Record audit	200
10. Job application fee	5	27. Room decoration	200
11. Late evening program	25	28. Snacks	5
12. Late morning program		29. Storage fee	5
(sleeping in)	20	30. Swimming pool	30
13. Letters (service fee)	5	31. Table games	10
14. Masking tape, 6 inches	10	32. Telephone call, 5 minutes	150
15. Matches, per book	15	33. Tub bath	50
16. Nap, afternoon	25	34. Visits, interhall	25
17. Outside trip	100	35. Youth Authority Board	
		report	300

ious objections to both psychotherapeutic and behavioral modalities in terms of their rehabilitative efficacy and research deficiencies. Instead, we emphasize the moral issues involved in their application within prisons.

One major objection can be raised in this regard with respect to both rehabilitative approaches. Both fail to develop their treatment within a rational standard of justice. Psychotherapeutic approaches such as the O. H. Close project, described earlier, have been repeatedly criticized along these lines by psychiatrist Thomas Szasz (1963) and more recently in the popular press by Jessica Mitford (1973). They and others have attacked the "Catch 22" moral logic of correctional treatment in which the therapist imposes his or her own set of therapeutic criteria on the prisoner with little or no regard for the moral legitimacy of the system as a whole, which traditionally extracts conformity to the rules under penalty of having one's parole denied. Thus, given the inmate's need to conform in order to win release, he or she often goes along with the treatment recommendations whether agreeing with them or not. The resulting arbitrariness is perhaps best illustrated by the following case witnessed by the authors at O. H. Close. When two youthful inmates were caught fighting, one received thirteen days' segregation by the staff in order "that he should think about his emotional immaturity" and the other (who actually instigated the fight) was directed to discuss his emotional immaturity with his social worker. These decisions were defended by the staff because of individual diagnostic and treatment information they had gathered on the two combatants. The fact that the fight had centered around a cell change unilaterally imposed by the administration and resulting in better accommodations for one at the expense of the other was not formally factored into the resolution. The staff members who made this decision strongly defended it to the authors on the grounds that it was "consistent" with the two boys' treatment plans.

The ethical problems in the behavior modification prison seem related more directly to the problems of the arbitrariness of the prison standards than to the capriciousness of individualized treatment decisions. In a behavioral prison, it is assumed that moral rightness is defined by the standards imposed by the institution and society, and inmates have points taken away for behaviors defined as antisocial by the institution. For example, one report we analyzed explained how the prison sought to extinguish an inmate's aggressive behavior as follows:

> Cal is a seventeen-year-old Negro youth. He has a five-year history of contacts with the law, ranging from bicycle theft through grand theft, burglary, and assault. He was committed to [the youth prison] following a particularly vicious assault on a youth who was in the county juvenile facility with him. As the result of the assault, the attacked youth required extensive surgery. . . .
>
> Cal was required to carry a small, discharged, dry-cell battery around with him. Although harmless, this battery was to serve as a discriminative stimulus to remind him to break off the behavioral sequence of events when he felt himself getting upset. Staff decided that points were insufficient to motivate this young man, so a variety of tangible reinforcers (such as soda) were brought into play for contract performance. He was requested to record the number of threatening remarks he made to others and then to work at reducing this number.

In another example, an inmate named James was made to accept a contract because he insisted on calling his youth supervisor a "white oppressor pig." The report recommending this contract suggested that James was using the rhetoric of black power to manipulate both counselors and wards. The behavioral contracts imposed on Cal and James emerged not from a reciprocal and mutual understanding with the inmates that their actions were wrong but rather from a unilateral staff decision that such behaviors were "antisocial" and needed to be extinguished. From the viewpoint of cultural relativity, this position is legitimate: Every society has the right to impose its standards on all its members. From the viewpoint of social justice, however, such unilateral decisions originate with a socially arbitrary set of norms, perhaps not shared or even understood by the inmates.

The moral incongruities in the psychotherapeutic and behavior modification approaches led us to consider another approach to learning and change, namely developmental theory. In this, we hoped we would find a theoretical approach that would be effective in changing prisoners and yet avoid the ethical inconsistencies of the other approaches.

Developmental Theory of Piaget and Kohlberg

The developmental theory of Piaget and Kohlberg provides an educational model consistent with the ideals of a democratic prison. Developmental theory is perhaps best embodied in the work of Jean Piaget and Lawrence Kohlberg. The key to developmental theory is a conception of the child's developing social intelligence in which it is suggested that through play and games the child comes to imitate or take on specific social roles and thereby learn the relationships among and between self and others. Socialization therefore is thought to represent a cooperative social effort in which mature selves increasingly take the part of others and move toward greater social consciousness, interdependence, and justice.

According to Piaget (1960), the child's conception of *natural* and *social* events evolves in four stages, and although experience may affect the rate of developmental change, the sequence itself is held to be *invariant*.

The stages are as follows:

Stage 1. The young infant at the *sensorimotor* stage has not yet discovered that objects continue to exist after they are beyond the limits of sight. When a ball leaves the infant's field of vision, for the infant it has disappeared.

Stage 2. At about eighteen months, the child progresses to what Piaget calls the *preoperational* stage in thinking, in which symbols become meaningful: A "ball" is no longer simply a blob of rubber with only physical meaning—it becomes symbolic of a larger context.

Stage 3. At about age five to seven, the child enters the stage of *concrete operations*, during which he or she develops the ability to think according to fixed, rule-bound ways of ordering reality; the child also moves toward greater logical objectivity.

Stage 4. During preadolescence or adolescence, the child achieves the stage of *formal operational* thought: He or she begins to systematically weigh logical propositions and to scientifically control for possible explanatory variables.

Consistent with this theory of intellectual development, Piaget ([1932] 1965) postulates that the understanding of *moral* rules also evolves through stages of development. Interviewing children from Switzerland, Piaget found three discrete stages of children's understanding of the rules of playing marbles.

Stage 1. The first "rules," found in children under age six, Piaget labels morally *egocentric*. Paralleling the preoperational stage, children *pretend* to follow parts of the rules of the older children but really do not play by any fixed rules.

Stage 2. Next, in children aged six to ten, is what Piaget calls the stage of *moral heteronomy* rules or the *morality of constraint*. Rules at this stage have an almost sacrosanct quality. If a rule is adopted by the older children, it is presumed to be "right." Marble rules for concrete operational children are obeyed to the letter. For instance, if a marble even touches a line, it is declared out, even if this means that no one wins the game. Even dysfunctional rules are obeyed by children at this stage of reasoning.

Stage 3. Parallel to the formal operational stage (ages eleven and above), this stage is called the stage of *moral autonomy*. Here rules are considered to be intentional social creations for the benefit of the group.

Kohlberg (1969, 1972, 1971) refined and elaborated Piaget's preliminary work and, like Piaget, emphasized the *process* of moral reasoning rather than its content. The theory likewise assumes a hierarchy of legal and moral adequacy. Unlike relativistic theories, there is an assumption of moral and legal evolution, with some social orders progressing further than others.

The theory also proposes that as the child matures in moral development he or she progressively reconsiders what is right as well as the relationship between law and society. Table 3 should serve to clarify. Kohlberg and his colleagues have postulated that for each moral stage a *necessary but not sufficient logical capacity* is required. For example, to attain Stage 3 a child requires "low-level" formal operations (Colby, 1973). This does not mean, however, that attaining a specific logical stage ensures that a particular moral stage will also be achieved. For example, some individuals possessing full formal operations may remain at Stage 2 in moral development.

Kohlberg's theory suggests that social institutions are critical in determining individual moral development, and studies by Thrower (1971) indicate that children raised in authoritarian environments such as orphanages and deprived of normal emotional attachments tend to have normal cognitive development but fail to mature in moral development. In contrast, a study by Reimer (1977) indicates that a positive social experiment on an Israeli kibbutz (characterized by intensive democratic support and participation) might speed up development. They found teenagers who moved during adolescence to be markedly more advanced in moral development than did age mates who remained in an Israeli slum environment. In general, institutions that encourage open dialogue, moral conflict, and democratic interaction are associated with rapid sociolegal development (Kohlberg, 1969). That is, they foster more mature understanding of social organizations and law. For example, individuals placed in positions where they are responsible for the maintenance of group and institutional norms develop more quickly than do others, because they are forced to examine the moral position of others.

Kohlberg's empirical evidence for the validity of his stage sequence comes from two sources. First, he cites evidence from both cross-sectional and longitudinal studies that suggests that people do move through the stages in order. Cross-sectional data indicate that in many different cultures—England, France, Israel, Taiwan, Turkey,

Table 3. Classification of Moral Judgment into Levels and Stages of Development.

Levels	Basis of Moral Judgment	Stages of Development
I	Moral value resides in external, quasi-physical happenings, in bad acts, or in quasi-physical needs rather than in persons and standards.	*Stage 1.* Obedience and punishment orientation. Egocentric deference to superior power or prestige, or a trouble-avoiding set. Objective responsibility. *Stage 2.* Naively egoistic orientation. Right action is that instrumentality satisfying the self's needs and occasionally others'. Awareness of relativism of value to each actor's needs and perspective. Naive egalitarianism and orientation to exchange and reciprocity.
II	Moral value resides in performing good or right roles, in maintaining the conventional order and the expectancies of others.	*Stage 3.* Good-boy orientation. Orientation to approval and to pleasing and helping others. Conformity to stereotypical images of majority or natural role behavior, and judgment by intentions. *Stage 4.* Authority and social-order maintaining orientation. Orientation to "doing duty" and to showing respect for authority and maintaining the given social order for its own sake. Regard for earned expectations of others.
III	Moral value resides in conformity by the self to shared or shareable standards, rights, or duties.	*Stage 5.* Contractual legalistic orientation. Recognition of an arbitrary element or starting point in rules or expectations for the sake of agreement. Duty defined in terms of contract, general avoidance of violation of the will or rights of others, and majority will and welfare. *Stage 6.* Conscience or principle orientation. Orientation not only to actually ordained social rules but to principles of choice involving appeal to logical universality and consistency. Orientation to conscience as a directing agent and to mutual respect and trust.

Source: Kohlberg, 1969, p. 376.

and Mexico's Yucatan—older children as a group were more mature in their thinking than were younger children (Kohlberg, 1971). In isolated societies, Kohlberg found development is far slower than it is in modern society. For example, most American adolescents are at conventional stages of reasoning (Stages 3 and 4). By contrast, Turkish adolescents remain at preconventional stages (Stage 1 or 2) longer. And, whereas in modern societies leaders tend to be at the principled level of moral reasoning, in small, isolated villages even the elders may not reach Stage 2 or 3.

Kohlberg also argues that each higher stage offers a philosophically more adequate means of resolving moral conflict and has attempted to demonstrate (at least through Stage 5) how each higher stage resolves ethical contradictions evident at earlier stages. He argues that the Stage 5 "legalistic" position offers an ethical perspective unavailable at the less-mature Stage 4 law-and-order orientation. For example, a predominantly Stage 4 individual asked to resolve a hypothetical dilemma in which a man, Heinz, must steal if he is to save his wife's life typically resorts to categorical answers:

Pro: You should steal it. If you did not do anything you'd be letting your wife die, it's your responsibility if she dies. You have to take it, with the idea of paying the druggist later.

Con: It is a natural thing for Heinz to want to steal. He still knows he's stealing and taking a valuable drug from the man who made it.

By contrast, the Stage 5 subject is able to distinguish moral blame because of the intent behind breaking the rule from the legal necessity not to make exceptions to rules.

Pro: The law wasn't set up for these circumstances. Taking the drug in this situation isn't really right, but it's justified to do so.

Con: You can't completely blame someone for stealing, but extreme circumstances don't really justify taking the law in your own hands. You can't have everyone stealing whenever they get desperate. The end may be good, but the ends don't justify the means.

A study of moral reasoning about the issue of capital punishment (Kohlberg and Elfenbein, 1976) finds a striking relationship between one's position on capital punishment and moral stage. Young children tended to believe in the justice of capital punishment. Later development, according to Kohlberg, reveals a series of flip-flops in orientation—for example, most Stage 3 subjects favored leniency, and Stage 4 supported capital punishment, but most of those beyond Stage 4 were opposed to the death penalty. The relationship of moral reasoning to choice on the issue of capital punishment is especially persuasive in the contrast between conventional and postconventional subjects. Fully 36 percent of Kohlberg's Stage 4 subjects favored capital punishment, whereas none of the later-stage subjects did.

The relationship of moral *reasoning* to moral *action* is even more complicated. Several studies have indicated at least some correspondence between reasoning and moral action. Krebs (1967) found a positive correlation between *not* cheating in an experimental situation and being a higher stage. Stage 2 children, he found, cheated far more often than did Stage 3 and 4 children in the same situation. Similarly, in the Milgram (1963) obedience study, experimenters ordered subjects to give increasingly severe shocks to a "stooge learner" (implying that an authority figure ordered a person to harm an innocent person). Clearly, only principled subjects might question the authority's right to inflict pain, and, as expected, 75 percent of a small group (eight persons) of the morally principled subjects refused. In comparison, only 43 percent of the remaining subjects refused. Another study, by Haan, Smith, and Block (1968), of activist protesters at Harvard and Berkeley, found that students in transition between conventional and principled thinking as well as principled moral thinkers (Stages 4½, 5, 6) were far more likely to take part in activist protests involving justice issues than were conventionally reasoning students (Stages 3-4).

These studies indicate that moral reasoning is associated with political and ethical action but they are ambiguous as to whether moral reasoning is associated with *individual* moral action. Obviously, any moral action involves more than simply knowing what is right in a specific situation. Fear, group pressure, cowardice, lack of will, or panic might prevent even a Stage 5 individual from doing what he or she understands is right in a specific situation. Still, these studies of capital punishment and the Berkeley sit-ins indicate that unless a person possesses specific moral capacities he or she simply will not know the right thing to do in specific situations involving complex and conflicting claims. And when "legal" authorities tell a person to do something illegal or immoral, as in the case of My Lai or Watergate, that person needs more than conventional reasoning to arrive at reasoned resolution. Although he or she may *not* act morally, a principled person at least has the capacity to act justly in a complex world of conflicting moral allegiances and convictions.

Kohlberg's work has not been received uncritically; one criticism deals with the issue of *cultural relativity,* which implies that the norms and values of a particular society may be judged only from that particular historical or cultural vantage point. From this perspective, it follows that there are neither universally valid ethical principles nor moral or legal standards that might be said to obligate all societies. An extreme example is found in the argument of a Brazilian judge, who, on freeing three back-country Amazon men who had killed a group of travelers, stated that for these people in their society killing was deemed to be morally correct. As opposed to cultural relativity, Kohlberg argues that there are universal ethical principles that have philosophic validity in any societal context.

Kohlberg is also criticized on the issue of the *invariance* of moral development; that is, his assertion that moral development *necessarily* moves from one stage to the next, a claim based on his sample of fifty-six men living during one historical epoch. Behavioral psychologists have suggested as an alternative hypothesis that the apparent evolution of moral thinking may be related to the contingencies in the environment rather than to a necessary evolution of logic. For instance, a child moving from the rewards of a controlling parent, to the exchanges of "chum" relationships, to the peer norms of the clique may move from Stage 1 to Stage 2 to Stage 3, as Kohlberg describes, but this movement may not result from developmental, logical necessity. Rather, it may result from the successive rewards of a changing environment, and under other conditions development might assume quite a different pattern.

Even some of Kohlberg's associates have doubted the extent to which the claim of invariance might be considered proven. John

Gibbs (1972), for example, suggests that, while there is rather substantial evidence to support an invariant sequence for the first four stages of Kohlberg's moral development theory, the evidence is less clear for Stages 5 and 6.

Developmental Theory and Delinquency

Kohlberg's theory has been tied to the problem of delinquency by a series of studies indicating that juvenile delinquents on the whole tend to be less morally and legally mature than nonoffenders are. A study by Kohlberg and Freundlich (1972) compared delinquents of different ages with nondelinquents from comparable social environments and found that the delinquents tended to be markedly less mature. For example, whereas only 16 percent of the delinquents in the sample were reasoning at conventional levels, over 70 percent of the nondelinquents attained at least a Stage 3 level of moral thinking. This conclusion does not mean that being at a lower stage in any single case *causes* delinquency, but it does suggest that most known delinquents are drawn from less morally mature youth. In addition, the consequences of being labeled *delinquent* may lead offenders to being contained in poor moral environments (such as foster care or prison). These findings are especially important when we consider that some delinquents reason much like children five years younger than themselves. For example, Kohlberg and Freundlich suggest that delinquents from fifteen to seventeen have a mean moral maturity much like a ten- or twelve-year-old middle-class child.

To illustrate the lag in the moral as well as legal reasoning of delinquents let us offer two examples of delinquent moral reasoning collected in a follow-up study of so-called hardened juvenile delinquents. Sam, sixteen, was scored as a mixture of Stage 1 and Stage 2 based on a moral judgment interview. In response to the dilemma (mentioned earlier) dealing with whether a husband should steal a drug if his wife was dying of cancer and it was the only way he could save her, Sam responded, "No, he shouldn't. That's stealing. I wouldn't do no time for nobody, no matter what. I don't care if it was my wife. It doesn't matter. . . . He will get *bagged* if he does that." His reasoning here fails to differentiate even rational interests from a fear of punishment. Similarly, when asked what a husband owes his wife, Sam said, "Well, you get married and shit and make all these promises and stuff, like to obey and you put on a ring and promise to listen, but you are just saying it." Similarly, when asked if a druggist could charge an exorbitant amount for a drug, Sam said he could charge what he wanted provided there was no law against it, indicating little awareness of the druggist's moral responsibility or of the rights of the wife.

Asked if the judge had the right to sentence him for "so much time" for such a small crime, Sam responded that "The judge could do what he wanted to do. He was the judge. He did it." Sam seemed to have no conception of the obligation of the judge to follow any specific laws, nor any conception that he, Sam, had any legal rights that would be protected by society. He also had little concept of why laws exist; when asked why society has laws against stealing, Sam replied, "It's to save the average Joes in society money, you know, things they wanr." Similarly, when asked if he should be punished for stealing from stores, Sam offered, "Well, the judge wanted me in jail." When asked if he knew what the U.S. Constitution said, he replied, "I was absent from school the day they talked about that."

Kohlberg's theory offers an ideological interpretation of delinquency dramatically different from psychotherapeutic and behavioral approaches. Psychotherapy assumes that matters of right and wrong are defined by society. Thus, Freud and his followers define moral conscience by the strength of the superego, the superego being an irrational force imposed early on the child by society through the parent. Because of the irrational nature of the superego, criminal behavior is viewed as a matter of psychological disease, rather than as an issue of justice. The criminal is sick, rather than bad, and should be treated rather than punished.

Behaviorism also assumes that what is right depends on the approved behaviors in a particular society. In this view, criminality is learned through the same process of conditioning as are normal behaviors. For example, a delinquent youth is rewarded by peers (and possibly parents) for stealing, just as other youths are for holding a job. Behaviorists hold that offenders can unlearn criminal behaviors much as they learn them. By reinforcing or rewarding positive behaviors (such as punctuality, good school performance, cleanliness), it is held that the offender may learn a new set of noncriminal actions.

In contrast, Kohlberg asserts that only universal—that is, non-culturally relative—moral principles may be used to judge particular actions. He offers that each sequential stage offers a mode of moral decision making more differentiated and integrated than are earlier stages. Thus, a Stage 4 position is "better" than a Stage 3 argument in that it considers the perspective of the social order as well as that of the peer group or of the informal norms of the culture. Similarly, a Stage 5 argument considers abstract principles of justice ("rightness") apart from the concrete Stage 4 proscriptions of the civil law. This hierarchy should be valid from any cultural perspective Kohlberg,holds, if its members consider each other's moral claims equitably with their own.

Kohlberg believes that his position provides a more rational philosophical basis for democratic action than do either psychotherapeutic or behavioral psychologies. Properly used, he says, it avoids the charge of indoctrination implicit in behaviorism, which justifies changing specific behaviors as being valued by and workable in the particular society.

Applied to the problem of delinquency, developmental theory provides a unique means of judging delinquent actions for instead of looking at a social action in terms of the norms of a particular society, we may view moral actions in terms of philosophically defensible ethical principles. Thus, a thief is judged in terms of the violation of the rational rights of others, rather than in terms of the specific laws or norms of a particular society. The theory also provides means of understanding psychological changes in an offender in terms of philosophical reasonableness rather than in terms of socially relativistic standards of adjustment psychology or behavioral control. Finally, the theory suggests mechanisms of psychological change that enhance the use of democratic processes within prison.

In the next chapter, we describe how we used developmental theory in an experimental effort to influence prison inmate moral thinking.

3

Stimulating
Moral Development

There are obviously major differences between conceptualizing educational theories and applying them in reality. Interventions rarely conform to their initial assumptions, and an intervention should change theory as theory must guide reform. When, in 1970, we began our first prison intervention at the Connecticut Correctional Institution at Cheshire, a maximum-security prison for young men, we had a psychological theory that had barely been tested in schools, much less prisons. The first educational work using Kohlberg's theory was conducted by Moshe Blatt, an Israeli doctoral student at the University of Chicago and a teacher in a local Hebrew school. Blatt hypothesized to Kohlberg that, by engaging students in socratic moral discussions about biblical topics, he could "raise" the moral reasoning of his students. Kohlberg at first did not think this was possible, believing at that time that his moral stages were broad products of social experience and were not readily amenable to educational intervention. Nevertheless, Blatt instituted his project, engaging his twelve- to fourteen-year-old Hebrew school students in a twelve-week course in which a variety of moral dilemmas were discussed. At the end of the program, the students were found to have changed more than an average of one-half of a moral stage. In a later study (Blatt and Kohlberg, 1973), the degree of change was somewhat reduced, to an average gain of one-third of a moral stage. Dowell (1972), Kohlberg (1978), and Mosher and Sullivan (1978) reported similar findings, using similar procedures. Moreover, the gains attained by the Blatt students were maintained, compared to students in a control group, more than two years after the intervention. This indicated that the discussion programs induced something more substantial than a superficial moral language and stimulated genuine shifts in the structure of moral reasoning.

In applying Blatt's methodology to prisons, we saw ourselves offering inmates a radically different therapy from any that existed then. However, instead of seeking to gain insight into the inmates' "hang-ups" or changing their "antisocial behavior," we sought to stimulate their conception of their moral relationships with their friends, family, and peers. We hoped to offer a new therapy based on the ideals of the socratic dialogue rather than on those of the "depth" psychology of Freud or the "mechanistic" behaviorism of Watson or Skinner.

Experiments at Cheshire

When we began our efforts, penology was in a wave of the post-1960s (and pre-Attica) infatuation with the promise of prison rehabilitation. It was believed that the prison could be humanized and criminal lives could be altered if only inmates could be offered "treatment" instead of simply being locked in custody.

The Cheshire reformatory was a typical punitive-custody youth prison, housing 425 inmates in the familiar tier arrangement and in an "honor" unit. During the summer of 1970, we selected forty inmates for participation in the study. Almost the entire institution had volunteered, probably because, as one inmate put it, "It sounds more interesting than stamping license plates or mopping floors." The program was implemented by randomly establishing a twenty-inmate experimental group, divided into two discussion sections of ten inmates each, who met separately for 36 two-hour sessions (3 sessions per week). In addition, a control group of twenty inmates was selected. All sessions were taped and transcribed. At the outset, we wondered whether a group of inmates would be willing seriously to discuss "abstract" moral dilemmas, but we happily found the inmates soon became genuinely interested in the process. Their interest was indicated by the fact that there were few obviously bored inmates and few unexplained absences (the average was less than one absence per subject).

The discussions began with our posing hypothetical dilemmas to the group. Over a period of a few weeks, a sense of group trust emerged that permitted the open discussion of personal issues. Inmates began to show more supportive behavior toward one another outside the discussion meetings, as we show later on. They also voluntarily submitted to the leaders real-life dilemmas they had encountered, both in prison, as well as on the streets. One, for example, suggested that the group discuss a dilemma about another inmate seeking prison favors by "ratting out" (informing on) other inmates. Another asked if it was right to intervene if an inmate knew a homosexual rape was in progress.

An example of how a dilemma might be discussed is as follows. It was introduced by an inmate who had faced the experience of being turned away by his parents while on the run from the police. The debate centered on whether it was right for parents to turn away their outlaw offspring if they knew he was wanted by the police. One of us, Joseph Hickey, framed the issue this way:

Hickey: Let's suppose you are living at home, and you start getting into trouble. And they try to talk to you and tell you not to get into trouble, but you are not listening—a few cars stolen, and B and E's [breaking and entering]—little stuff [laughter], but you haven't been pinched yet. And your parents are getting pretty upset; they figure that the day of arrest is coming. They are picking it up that you are getting into trouble—school reports. What should they do?

Zeke: Leave you alone. Before they do anything, they should leave you alone.

Al: They should ship you out of the country.

Hickey: Leave you alone?

Zeke: You will never be able to look at the problems in life if you
           got Mommy and Daddy fronting for you. And if they call
           the police and you get busted it is best to just leave you
           alone.
Al: What should they do? Kick you in the ass and throw you
           out on the street?
Phil: If they pick you up in the street, they are creating this other
           problem, because then you feel rejected. So I think they
           should turn you in to the police, because if they don't you
           are going to do something else, and you are going to try
           and hide behind Mommy and Daddy if it happened
           again. . . . If you feel that your mother and father are on
           your side, that is all the more reason to go back out there
           and do something. But if they turn you in to the police or
           kick you out into the street, then you are rejected; so now
           you got a problem . . .
Al: You are going to feel rejected if they call the police?
Hickey: Hold it. There seem to be two strains of argument here.
           [One is] "Do nothing, and let him take care of himself."
           The other argument is "What does a parent owe the kid?"
           And the argument seems to be that you have to cut loose
           with the parents; you've got to do your own thing. So they
           shouldn't do anything to the kid, or, if they do anything,
           they should let the kid make his own rules?
Al: No. The best thing for a parent to do is throw him out.
Zeke: If they throw him out, he can go to some other people and
           stay there.
Phil: First of all, the mother and father care about the son, be-
           cause you don't just raise a kid and then throw him out.
Hickey: So you say if you throw him out, you are not really helping
           him?
Phil: You are not helping him at all.
Zeke: I look at it from the parent's point of view. You know, I
           would say to him, "I won't call the Man, but there's noth-
           ing I can do. If you want me to call the hospital or call the
           Man because that will be better for you, I will do that. But
           if you don't want me to do that, I won't."
Phil: That's like letting him get away with it.

Hickey: How is he going to learn?

Zeke: That's what you said before. He's got to learn to stand on his own two feet.

Phil: And is he going to learn? You are saying it will help him be slick, help him get away with it. Help him beat that system, help him beat the law. That's what you're saying.

Jay: You don't need a prison to help a man think.

Al: It changed you. It changed me.

Jay: It didn't change *me*! *I* changed me! Not the prison. The prison did shit for me. *I* did it!

Hickey: Hold it. Let's have it one at a time because we're going around in a vicious circle. Let's get back with you, Zeke.

Zeke: I think if the parents get along all right, they both showed enough love for their kid, you know, and the kid knows that they love him, too. . . . Say they spank him or show him what's right and wrong and things at the beginning. When the kid gets older and he does something wrong and the parents try to straighten him out, he is gonna respect them.

Jay: Suppose you give this kid all the love, understanding, and goodies, and everything else that goes with being a good daddy and a good mommy—you give this dude everything—and then he goes back?

Al: Then it's time to quit. Then it's time for that son of a bitch to do something for himself.

This particular discussion continued with a great deal of argument but with no apparent resolution. The two Stage 2 inmates argued that the parents don't owe their children much and the best therapy for them was a "quick kick in the ass." The Stage 3 inmates, Phil and Zeke, argued that the delinquent youth might feel rejected by his parents if he was turned in. The discussion leader, Hickey, sought to make the moral issues in the case as salient as possible and continually asked the inmates to articulate the reasons underlying their opinions. He also attempted to keep the discussion focused on a specific issue and to maintain a positive, supportive tone among the discussants.

As the sessions progressed, there was a marked shift in the content and process of the discussions. Increasingly, the hypothetical dilemmas emerged directly from the immediate lives of the inmates. For example, when an inmate named Charlie returned from a "vacation in the box" (the punitive segregation cell) for fighting with another inmate, Hickey raised the dilemma of how Charlie would react if his cell were ripped off by the prison officers. The discussion went as follows:

Hickey: Let's take a very specific situation like, we all leave here at 11:30 A.M., and you go back to your cells, and you find that the cell block has been ripped off again—there's been "general inspection." Jim finds his papers and stuff all over the floor. What are you going to do?

Charlie: I am going to get hostile, and I am going down to the frigging desk, and I am going to grab somebody. . . . They had no business touching them. In the first place, they are pictures of my people [family photographs]. And, in the second place, I don't like anybody putting their hands on something that's mine, without authorization. I don't dig it, and I don't know how else to put it: I don't dig it, man.

Hickey: You really don't dig it—I think everybody would agree with you [laughter]. Now the question is "Does everybody agree with your reaction?"

Hal: Actually, you overreacted to the thing because there ain't that much you can do about it.

Terry: What?

Charlie: I can go down and square that dude's [the officer's] jaw.

Clint: You won't do that. You're just fronting.

Charlie: I am serious. You can do it; but you can get in a whole lot of trouble for it too!

Hickey noted that Charlie shouldn't feel "like his ass is out in the open, because everyone needs someone." After the 11:30 lunch bell rang, signaling the end of the session, Charlie summed up by indicating his profound disappointment in his behavior: "The bad part of me is a cover-up, like 'Fuck you,' you know, 'Beat it, I don't need you.' But inside, 'Help me,' you know. . . . Inside I need friends, I need people. I am changing, and, like, I think everybody is subject to change. And, like . . . some people change when something happens to them, whereas other people . . . it takes a long time for some people to change, a long time, and it took me a long time to see where I have finally wanted to go and finally see that everything I have done in the past has done nothing but fuck me around."

While this type of apparent self-revelation is common in conventional group therapy, our approach to Charlie's problems was conceptually different from that of traditional prison psychotherapy programs.

First, Charlie's response to anger was seen as a moral issue for the group rather than a matter of Charlie's supposed neurotic personality. The inmates and Hickey sought to make Charlie aware of the ethical implications of his behavior. For example, Charlie was asked about the consequences to his girlfriend of his violent temper, the issue being posed as one of fairness. By contrast, a psychoanalytically trained therapist would have focused more on the inner motives or causes producing his angry outbursts.

Second, our approach put more emphasis on the group's attaining a sense of community than a conventional group psychotherapy program would have. The development of an autonomous moral community was seen as a critical goal. Charlie's "conversion" served as much as a means of bringing the group together as of fostering understanding through insight.

Third, the leader's role differs from that seen in traditional psychotherapy programs. Instead of offering the inmate professional therapeutic advice, "Charlie, I see you acting violently as a front for your basic insecurity," the leader sought to create a climate in which the inmates could form a mutual contract to aid one another. In one session, the leader looked a rather fierce inmate in the eye and asked point-blank: "John, do you care about Rog?" The answer being affirmative, the leader asked Rog if he cared about John. With each inmate admitting publicly that he cared what happened to the other, help emerged naturally from the group instead of being dispensed by the paid professional. In most cases, inmate-to-inmate advice was not only more accurate but was accepted with greater psychological force than would have been the case had the leaders made a similar observation.

In final sessions, there was increased group interest in the topic of injustice in the prison as well as in the larger society. For example, one inmate, Dan, amazed everyone by conducting a "sociological" survey of moral attitudes in the prison. He reported: "What I did was I asked ten different officers how inmates should act toward them and how they think they should act toward inmates. . . . Ten officers were asked this question, and they all agreed that not one answer could cover it fully. Nine said they had to be tolerant. Only one said he had to be hard. Eight said they had to be sympathetic. When asked if officers should respect inmates, four hesitated before answering."

Dan concluded with a plea for inmates and staff to work together for the inmates' release and success: "Society cannot understand why this person acts the way he does, so they send him to prison with the hope that he will straighten out. What society does not see is that what this person really wants is someone to notice him and accept him. Society rejects him as unfit, so there is nothing left for him to do. He feels again entirely in the wrong, just like in the reformatory. The prison system becomes easier to live in than in society, so he eventually becomes institutionalized."

The increased political consciousness of the group was demonstrated in other areas as well. When Mal was placed in punitive segregation by the discipline board for punching another youth, who happened to be the son of a state representative and who was believed by other inmates to have instigated the incident, the group appealed to the deputy warden, who reversed the decision. The group also organized a meeting of black and white inmate leaders to agree not to engage in the traditional prison pastime of homosexual rape of young inmates (called "punking") on the grounds that "Punking wasn't right, and it wasn't cool." In addition, the group members formed a committee to plan a halfway house, and with the help of Quinipiac College professor Barry Fritz their plans became a reality, with ex-inmates living together in a college dormitory.

Analysis of pre- and posttests revealed quite different thinking at the end of the twelve weeks of intervention as compared with the beginning. These differences were derived by administering two different sets of standard moral dilemmas, each set containing four situations similar in content to the following: "In Europe, a woman was near death from cancer. One drug might save her, a form of radium that a druggist in the same town had recently discovered. The druggist was charging $2,000, ten times what the drug cost him to make. The sick woman's husband, Heinz, went to everyone he knew to borrow the money, but he could only get together about half of what it cost. He told the druggist that his wife was dying and asked him to sell it cheaper or let him pay later. But the druggist said no. The husband got desperate and broke into the man's store to steal the drug for his wife. Should the husband have done that? Why?"

The subjects' responses to these dilemmas were evaluated using a complex scoring technique involving some twenty-five moral aspects, including conscience and property rights, that Kohlberg had identified by stage. Thus each moral stage had a corresponding set of prototypic responses for each moral aspect. By matching the subjects' responses against the prototypic responses, it was possible to identify a dominant stage of moral reasoning. Additionally, each stage was assigned 100 points called Moral Maturity Scores (MMS). A pure Stage 1 subject would theoretically earn 100 points, and a pure Stage 6 subject would score 600 moral maturity points. Typically, however, subjects scored between adjacent stages, which was reflected in terms of a dominant and a minor stage. Thus, a score of 4 (3) would represent an individual predominantly using Stage 4 reasoning on most aspects but with some Stage 3 usage on others. The moral maturity score in this case would range between 375 and 425.

For example, one inmate's pretest showed a mix between Stage 2 and Stage 3 thinking, and when confronted with the hypothetical dilemma of stealing drugs for a sick wife he initially showed little awareness of a full Stage 3 moral perspective. At the time, he said, "It depends on the feelings he has for her. If he cares for her, so he should steal it if he really cares. . . . If he doesn't care, however, let her die." The same inmate's posttest on which he scored between Stage 3 and 4 indicated a much more mature moral position. He was aware of the moral perspective of the law as well as that of the husband, the wife, and the druggist: "It's not right to steal, because there is a law against stealing. This here is a situation where it is necessary to steal. The druggist only paid $200 for the drug, and if he gave him $1,000 he wouldn't be losing anything. He couldn't lose anything, and his wife's life was on the line. It was necessary to steal the drug to save her life. Still, he broke the law, but the law should still take into consideration that his wife was dying. He asked him to take the $1,000 now. I look at it that the druggist was greedy."

Overall, six of the nineteen inmates in the experimental group changed in terms of their major or dominant stage of moral reasoning, an average of one-third of a stage, most of them from Stage 2 to 3. Other inmates shifted in terms of their dominant stage, and all of the inmates moving to Stage 3 possessed the requisite logical reasoning to move to this mode of thought. These inmates were more involved in the discussions and participated more frequently than the average member. Table 4 summarizes the changes between the pre- and post-tests of inmates exposed to the thirty-six moral discussion groups and of those who were not.

Table 4. Changes in Cheshire Inmates' Moral Reasoning after Twelve Weeks of Intervention.

	Stage					
	1	2	3	4	5 and 6	MMS
	Experimental Subjects					
Pretest	5.3	43.5	47.7	3.1	0.0	251.0
Posttest	3.2	37.9	47.8	10.7	0.0	268.0
	Control Subjects					
Pretest	5.0	51.0	36.0	6.0	3.0	250.8
Posttest	5.0	51.0	37.0	7.0	2.0	254.1

Note: $t = 2.62$; $p < 0.05$; 1 stage = 100 MMS points

Effect of the Prison Setting on Moral Change

Although we were pleased with the Cheshire inmates' response to the program, there was much about the program that troubled us. The inmates were genuinely excited about the discussion groups, but there seemed to be few opportunities for them to experiment with new moral behaviors. One case was particularly revealing in this respect. A hardened criminal at age eighteen, Richard had been abandoned as a child and had received his first major arrest, for assault, at age ten.

Between his tenth and eighteenth birthdays, he spent less than two years outside of prison. Six of his arrests involved assaulting a police officer. A parole agent said that Richard would stand on the street and a police officer would ask his name; "Ten minutes later you'd hear sirens, and it would take nine cops to get him to the station."

At the outset of our group sessions, Richard was a Stage 2 and hostile. In one meeting, for example, when asked if he would intervene if he saw a young girl trying to commit suicide, he responded, "What for? To fuck her?" As the sessions went on, however, he became more revealing about his life situation. He talked openly about his sense of failure and his fear of his violent temper. During the program, however, he began to control his temper better. Once, when about to "punch out" another inmate, he told the group that "I remembered what Hickey told me, 'Think where the other guy is coming from.' I let him slide." Although almost purely Stage 2 at the beginning of the program, offering on the pretest that "He would steal the drug if he needed his old lady," at the end of twelve weeks he scored a full stage higher. In the posttest, he argued, "You should steal to save the wife. He loved her like any husband should. The man oughta care about his lady. Any husband would care that much."

Richard himself also began to show signs of caring. Assigned to the boiler room, he found a stray cat and made it his pet, feeding it milk stolen from the cafeteria. One day he announced to the discussion group that the cat was the "First thing I ever really cared about." However, a prison edict mandated that all pets would have to be put to death, a not unreasonable order, since institutions are prone to animal-carried infections. When a correctional officer visited Richard in the boiler room and demanded the cat, however, he was immediately rendered unconscious on the floor, and four hours later Richard was in the state adult prison. Convicted of assault on an officer, Richard was given a three-year "overtime" sentence, to be served in a maximum-security prison. He is still in prison!

Richard's plight was paralleled by the fate of a number of the program participants. Follow-up interviews revealed a complex pattern. After two years in the community, roughly 40 percent of the inmates in the experimental program had returned to prison, compared to 55 percent of the control group. But few of even the successful (nonrecidivist) graduates had attained what they considered to be positive, happy lives. Both recidivists and nonrecidivists described their prison experience as overwhelmingly degrading. For example, one inmate offered: "The guards treated you like shit. You could sense it. And the administration, they put up phony images to the public to make themselves look good, and all the time they are in there killing people, taking a big chunk out of our life. And that's why 85 percent of the people (inmates) don't do nothing: They go in and out. It's a school for crime."

Failures seemed far too frequent to us, even when we were able to arrange a suitable parole plan, including a good job, as well as admission to college. Even the former Cheshire inmates who had "made it" affirmed that their success was in spite of, rather than as a product of, their jail experience. As one said: "Jail didn't rehabilitate me. I did. . . . It's not jail that does it; it is the release [from] jail. You can't rehabilitate in jail; you have to rehabilitate out of jail. So actually, rehabilitation in jail is a farce. It is out of jail that it is possible, but in jail there is no such word."

This experience of bitter failure seemed related to both the subjective and the objective injustice of prison. People who had been Cheshire inmates nearly universally rejected the moral order of the custody prison as unjust and arbitrary. Even the Stage 3 and 4 inmates tended to see most staff members as hostile, punitive, deceitful, and manipulative. When asked what purpose the prison served, one inmate offered, "It's here so the guards can earn a living." Most inmates tended to see relationships with other inmates in Stage 2 instrumental terms. Inmates were seen as "ripping off" each other, "ratting out" their friends, and "punking" weaker inmates. Relationships with other inmates were necessary for mutual protection; however, they were usually seen as marred by "fronting" (playing it cool). Fronting was necessary to defend one's interest and to "con" the guards and other inmates. The inmate world was, to use Hobbes's terms, a "war of all against all." In this hostile state, inmates recognized no generally agreed-on norms, nor were there fixed standards that actively regulated social relationships.

In prison, a social world that appeared brutal and exploitative, prisoners seemed to reason well below their highest possible stage of moral reasoning. To document this, we constructed a series of dilemmas that reflected moral conflicts experienced by inmates and guards. For example, one dilemma asked, "Should an inmate aid a young boy from his home town who was being shaken down for cigarettes by older inmates?" When inmate responses to the prison dilemmas were compared with those to the standard Kohlberg situations, it was found that they scored an average of one-fourth of a moral stage lower on the prison dilemmas than on the standard dilemmas. None of the inmates scored higher on the prison dilemmas than on the standard dilemmas.

This situational regression is illustrated by an inmate who scored a mixture of Stages 2 and 3 on the prison dilemmas and a mixture of Stages 3 and 4 on the standard Kohlberg dilemmas. When asked, on the Kohlberg standard, if he would steal a drug to save his dying wife, he responded he would "if the wife was sick and it was the only way to get it. . . . If he loves his wife, he shouldn't care about punishment. The right thing in his mind would be to steal it." However, when asked whether he would help a young man from his hometown who is being shaken down for cigarettes, he replied, "People from your town should be made to look 'cool.' If the guy is made to look like a punk, then the town looks bad. It's not so much the guy as the town. The older inmate will probably help the new inmate if he is stronger than the other guys. If he is weak, he'll just walk away."

This inmate's reasons for helping his dying wife depended both on a Stage 3 role relationship and on what sounds like a Stage 4 rule—that people who wish to live should be helped to do so. His reasoning on the prison situation was dramatically more nihilistic: Moral duty rests on a Stage 3 (or possibly Stage 2) notion of "making your town look good," a desire tempered by Stage 2 instrumental concerns as to whether or not he is tougher than the other inmates. In the larger societal dilemma, the inmate was willing to sacrifice all for his dying wife. In the world of prison, honor is subordinate to a kind of prison realpolitik.

These observations seemed related to both the sense of moral anomie experienced by many released prisoners and the prisons' high recidivism rate. It seemed to us, then, that unless the prison could be transformed from a "war of all against all" into a place with a common sense of community and concern little could be expected in the way of altered lives for inmates.

From Moral Education to Just Community

These observations forced us to reconsider our program. Initially, we had assumed that changes in moral thinking could be achieved within existing prisons and that changes might have a major impact on the lives of inmates after their release. Thus we decided, instead of trying to reform the prisoners, we would seek to change the prison. Only then could we hope to affect the inmate's moral reasoning.

We observed that almost all successful efforts at correctional therapy utilized the sense of common community as a central focus of the rehabilitative process—for example, the Maxwell Jones "therapeutic community." Synanon, the Black Muslims, the Jehovah's Witnesses, and the California Youth Authority (in its guided group interaction program) all utilized intentionally created and highly cohesive communities to help change their members.

The San Francisco-based Delancey Street Foundation is another such example. This unusual inmate-run community, which owns a communal residence, restaurant, auto shop, ad agency, and other enterprises, seeks to rehabilitate drug offenders by their living and working together. In Delancey Street, a deviation by a member is used by other members to provide an example of misconduct, which serves to rearticulate and reaffirm the community's values as well as to give the deviant a severe reprimand—called a "haircut"—by a community of peers. Charles Hampden-Turner (1977) describes the "haircut" of a man named Bryant, a supposedly reformed drug addict as follows.

> "I'd like to put the Game [meeting] on myself."
> "Did you hear an unpleasant noise?"
> "Something's crawled out from beneath a stone. It's rattling."
> "At least let me speak!" Bryant blazes. "How can you hope to do justice if you won't hear me."
> "Justice, ha! If you'd got what you deserved, you'd be fucking dead."
> "Let's hear him. Tell us why they shaved your head, Bryant."
> "I asked to have my head shaved." Bryant is quiet again and contrite. . . . There is a ripple of mock applause.

Then a black director leans forward in his chair and snarls, "You're so goddamn sanctimonious you make me puke! Even now with your head shaved you can't come clean. You cop but you don't cop. I doubt you're capable of truth anymore. You know and we know that mind-fucking a girl and playing bongo drums are not head-shaving offenses. As for pretending that you have to be a martyr to our disbelief, that is such fuckin' hypocrisy that I'm surprised your nose hasn't grown clear out of the window!"

"What's goin' on here?"

"Yeah, what's the background?"

Several people are asking for clarification. Bryant's "barber" reviews the events of the last year.

"Okay, you wanta hear the punk's progress? Bryant is one of our earliest residents. He was at Bush Street, where it all began. About a year ago his two roommates accused him of being loaded. That's not an easy thing for a roommate to do. They said he was scratchin', he was nodding off, and he watered his TV set instead of the azaleas.

"Well, we had an inquiry, and Bryant swore on his mother's grave and with tears in his eyes that he was clean. He begged us to uphold the pledged word of a brother against circumstantial evidence. We decided to believe him. We do that with our senior residents. Someone who is not believed cannot become credible to himself or others. Soon after that the rumors started. A guy we know on the outside talked to a dealer, and he gave a description of Bryant that was dead on. Another witness came forward who'd seen Bryant on the night in question and said he was definitely loaded. Finally his 'old lady' left him—couldn't stand the stench of lies around him, she said.

"So now we have this minicop, this utterly transparent pretense that he is punishing himself more severely than we would wish because he holds himself to higher standards. Trust Bryant to shave his head while trying to escape from the meaning of doing so!"

"Know why I resent you, Bryant?" One of Delancey's best business managers is into the ring.

"I resent the hell out of you college-educated middle-class fuck-ups. You're the real niggers, with your bongo drums, your tribal hats, and your protoculture, when the truth is you've maimed and crippled and worn down more black men and women than the biggest white bigot in this town. We uneducated slobs keep repeating to ourselves, 'gotta

educate our children and ourselves and prepare for the day.'
Then we look at you or Josh over there, and we think, 'Wait a
minute! I could graduate from college and still be a slave. I
could end up like Bryant—the most erudite liar that ever tied
himself in supersophisticated knots and used his brains
against his own life.' Ain't no one here believe you but
yourself!''

Bryant's "haircut" represents obviously something more than
simple group disapproval. It signifies more the spontaneous and yet
ritualized feeling of group commitment to a particular set of collective social norms. Rosabeth Moss Kanter (1972) observes that such
group confession rituals are perhaps essential to the functioning of
intensive and successful collectivist communities. Drawing on a
range of utopian experiences, such as the nineteenth-century communes of Oneida and New Harmony, she finds such public confessions and sanction to be a necessary ritual to solidify group commitment and sentiment. Only those communities that publicly enforce
their norms, she insists, are able to survive more than a single
generation.

Public confessions and reprimands help to solidify community values as well as to socialize members into the acceptable identity
norms of the group. Bryant's haircut, for instance, rallies the group
together, and it places pressure on him to express himself openly and
to give up the "junkie format." Cohesive communities also focus on
moral and metaphysical rebirth. The Black Muslims and Jehovah's
Witnesses, for example, all attempt to precipitate a "conversion"
experience as a core community ritual. They also offer their members
an accepting—although often humiliating and controlling—community that stimulates, welcomes, and gives social meaning to a new
life commitment.

One social theory useful in interpreting such intensive communities derives from Emile Durkheim. Individual morality, he
posited, is learned through a person's acceptance of group norms of a
collective. That is, morality is taught through the maintenance of
group norms. Thus, the punishment of unruly students, Durkheim
([1925] 1961) argued, rarely deters them or others from unruly acts.
However, *public* punishment serves well to articulate, exemplify, and
show respect for the rules of the group. Through exemplary punish-

ment, a teacher rallies support for the rules of the class, as well as punishes violations of the rules.

Anton Makarenko (1951), the Russian criminologist and educator, attempted to articulate and apply this type of approach in the context of Marxist educational theory. From 1923 to 1930, Makarenko was the director of a "reform school" for delinquents. When first assigned to the school, he found an unruly mob of angry youths. Over the years, however, he was able to instill both order and a sense of collective group feeling, and discipline—enforced by a "general council"—came to be considered a problem of group morale rather than the individual problem of a particular student. Makarenko believed that morality was best engendered by having a positive collectivity as a moral reference point for the child or adolescent. Punishment, therefore, was usually effected by praising behavior consistent with the public ideals of society (self-sacrifice, industriousness, and so on), and publicly criticizing actions defying such values. Urie Brönfenbrenner (1970) offers a powerful example of Makarenko's educational practice:

> Class 3-B is just an ordinary class; it's not especially well disciplined. The teacher has led this class now for three years, and she has earned affection, respect, and acceptance as an authority from her pupils. Her work is law for them.
>
> The bell has rung, but the teacher has not yet arrived. She has delayed deliberately in order to check how the class will conduct itself.
>
> In the class, all is quiet. After the noisy class break, it isn't so easy to mobilize yourself and to quell the restlessness within you! Two monitors at the desk silently observe the class. On their faces is reflected the full importance and seriousness of the job they are performing. But there is no need for them to make any reprimands: The youngsters with pleasure and pride maintain scrupulous discipline; they are proud of the fact that their class conducts itself in a manner that merits the confidence of the teacher. And she deliberately refrains from praising them for the quiet and order, since in their class it could not be otherwise.
>
> During the lesson, the teacher gives an exceptional amount of attention to collective competition between "links." (The links are the smallest unit of the Communist youth organization at this age level.) Throughout the entire

lesson, the youngsters are constantly hearing which link has best prepared its lesson, which link has done the best at numbers, which is the most disciplined, which has turned in the best work.

The best link not only gets a verbal positive evaluation but receives the right to leave the classroom first during the break and to have its notebooks checked before the others. As a result, the links received the benefit of collective education, common responsibility, and mutual aid.

"What are you fooling around for? You're holding up the whole link," whispers Kolya to his neighbor during the preparation period for the lesson. And during the break he teaches her how to better organize her books and pads in her knapsack.

"Count more carefully," says Olya to her girlfriend. "See, on account of you, our link got behind today. You come to me, and we'll count together at home."

The Delancey Street, Makarenko, and similar examples of intense cohesive communities offered methods we gradually understood to be critical to the process of successful moral renewal. We believed that it might be possible for us to use some of the mechanisms common to group cohesion therapies, but not necessarily adopt the collectivist assumptions of Makarenko or other approaches. Posed in terms of Kohlberg's theory, we sought to create a prison community that might have the cohesiveness and moral charisma associated with Stage 4 (social order) community but would operate according to Stage 5 principles of an open social contract and a persistent concern with due process and fairness. We hoped, in other words, to use some of the techniques of collective educational models but not necessarily accept their conventional, often moralistic assumptions.

Durkheim and Makarenko believed that people learn their moral ideas primarily through norm socialization process; that is, by internalizing the norms of the group. We hypothesized, however, that such intensive group experiences might force people to rethink the moral logic with which they solve moral problems. Thus, whereas Makarenko hoped to socialize the delinquent into new Marxist values, we sought to use the same means to place him or her in moral conflict. By having the delinquent take the perspective of the group as well as by having the group reacting to his behavior, we sought to create changes in the offenders' thinking and behavior.

This approach is consistent with Cooley (1912) and Mead's (1934) theory of social learning. In their view, a sense of morality derives directly from experiences in group life. For Mead, the learning of conscience emerged from the development of what he called the "generalized other," the internalization by the individual of the perspective of the group. According to Mead, when a person commits an act that violates the norms of the group, a part of his or her self views this action as the group might see it. For Mead and Cooley, the experience of intensive community life in which individuals empathized with and were interdependent with one another was essential to full social development. Such a "just community," we knew, would be in stark contrast to traditional prisons where role-taking opportunities are minimized, justice is administered to inmates by officials, and inmates are not allowed to become involved in prison affairs or engage in any kind of political activity.

Our shift from moral therapy to the idea of a "just community" represented a substantial change in emphasis. We had entered the Cheshire project as psychologists, albeit moral psychologists. Six months later, we saw our role as interveners dedicated to reforming the basic structure and conception of prison. By the spring of 1971, the goal of moral therapy was at best a secondary interest. What we wanted to do was change prisons.

We resolved to find a correctional system that would allow us to try to change one of its prisons so it would allow the development of such a just community as we have described here. Of course, we understood that few prisons would allow such a program. One of the presumed lessons of the history of penal reform is that such efforts usually are short-lived and ineffective. Our effort to prove this "lesson" wrong is the topic of the following chapter.

4

Establishing Self-Government in Prisons

Finding prison administrators prepared to accept the risks implicit in our experiment, which we called the "Just Community" program, was not an easy matter. We were refused entry to a work camp in a southern state and to a youth facility in New England. A top administrator reacted to what we thought was an eloquent presentation of our ideas by commenting, "We talked over what you fellows had to say during the break and figure we can divide it all into three parts. The first part we are already doing. The second part we couldn't understand. The third part we thought was pure bullshit."

Finally, Connecticut's state correctional commissioner, John R. Manson, asked us to meet with the administrative staff of a women's prison, the correctional center at Niantic. The institution had experienced a serious disturbance just prior to his appointment as commissioner, and he felt that it was in need of some fundamental change. Manson's deputy commissioner for female services, Janet

York, who also acted as superintendent at Niantic, agreed with his assessment and urged us to visit the facility.

During the initial meetings, York and her staff presented an extremely candid overview of the facility and its problems, emphasizing the traditional indifference toward women's prisons in general and underscoring the need for sound programming and appropriate administrative changes. Impressed by their willingness to give new ideas a fair hearing and assist in every way possible toward their implementation, we in turn presented an overview of our theoretical assumptions, asked numerous questions about the institution, and offered to lend whatever assistance we could. We had learned about the importance of administrative support during our experiences at Cheshire. Although we had received the enthusiastic approval of then commissioner Ellis MacDougall, Manson's predecessor, lower-echelon administrators were less committed to our work or even resentful of it and often made implementation of our ideas difficult. As a result, we knew that any future programs would require not only the approval of top administrators but also active support at the institutional level. After reaching an initial agreement with York, we set about to define an acceptable entry point and the guidelines under which the work would be accomplished.

Niantic Correctional Center

The Niantic Correctional Center is spread out over a thousand acres of beautiful Connecticut countryside, and the overall impression is of a small New England college campus. Inmates are housed in five attractive brick buildings and there are some dozen additional buildings for education, administration, chaplain, prison industries, and staff housing. However, since these buildings were constructed over a forty-year time span, without any overall plan, they present certain administrative problems in the management of the institution. Faulty plumbing, wiring, and heating systems, for example, are compounded by the fact that no two buildings were constructed with interchangeable equipment. This situation strains an already overworked and underbudgeted maintenance force, leaving no time for capital improvements or structural alterations necessary for ongoing institutional vitality.

In addition, there was a lack of professional expertise among the staff, although the institution clearly espoused a treatment posture. The superintendent was a trained social worker with considerable experience, but only a few of her assistants had formal training in the correctional helping services. And there was a high staff turnover rate. The prison industry program at Niantic also presented a source of stress. For years, Niantic's major inmate industry was an extensive farming operation, but the farm ultimately was deemed "uneconomical" and discontinued, idling a large number of inmates and burdening other work, educational, and residential areas.

Perhaps the key dilemma, however, for the institution was the rapid shift in racial makeup of the inmate population. Until the early 1960s, Niantic's inmates had been largely white, as was the staff, and the social norms of the institution had reflected white middle-class values: grace at mealtime, properly set dinner table, an emphasis on orderliness and punctuality, and concern for "proper, ladylike attire." By 1970, however, the racial makeup of the inmates had shifted dramatically as more inner-city blacks were sent to Niantic, and they found much of the institution's atmosphere unacceptable and even threatening.

None of these problems were so overwhelming as to cause the major disturbance that had occurred shortly before our arrival. In May 1970, nearly all the black residents of one of the more troublesome living units staged a sit-down strike in the unit dining room and demanded a meeting with the superintendent. This action triggered a sympathy riot by some twenty-nine problem inmates, mostly black, in the North Building, the prison's maximum security unit. The administration elected not to negotiate, and a team of state troopers and corrections officers were hastily assembled. Equipped with Mace and riot clubs, the troopers waded into the demonstrators. When it was over, some seventeen battered women inmates were bussed under armed guard to a nearby jail and placed in punitive segregation. For the next several days, female guards sent from Niantic to supervise the rioters were subjected to verbal and physical threats such as they had never experienced. Some of the officers retorted in kind. After their return to Niantic, no one could doubt that a serious problem existed between the black and white inmates. At the institution neither group was talking to the other, and many feared another confrontation. The catalytic agent for this riot was the manner in which inmates were assigned to the various living units, a so-called graded cottage system. This system was instituted to provide "properly motivated" inmates with a means of moving to cottages that gave them more privileges and independence, until they arrived at the "honor house," where they were granted such privileges as unsupervised visits, frequent furloughs, and work releases. The problem was that, given the middle-class orientation of the institution, the most "difficult" inmates were usually black and never got beyond the lowest-grade cottages, whereas when the riots occurred the vast majority of the honor house dwellers were white and of often middle-class or even upper-class backgrounds. This exacerbated the alienation felt by black inmates and fostered a perception of injustice as well as prejudice on the part of the staff. A well-intentioned program aimed at helping the inmates thus unwittingly provided the catalyst for a major racial disturbance.

The Intervention Strategy

Given this state of affairs, we determined our immediate task was to resolve the "Mexican standoff" as one lieutenant described it between staff and black inmates. To accomplish this, it was imperative that we maintain neutrality. In short, we decided our program should operate in such a way that it would be perceived by inmates and staff as fair and just; that the legitimate needs of all participants should not be arbitrarily subordinated in the name of custody and control on the one hand and black liberation rhetoric on the other. Our roles as unpaid consultants aided this objective admirably. The first move toward resolving the standoff was to organize a series of open-ended weekly meetings conducted by ourselves, in which we would listen to complaints and would introduce, we hoped, our ideas about democracy. Staff were invited first. Because he had considerable experience, which provided him with a sense of the perspective of the line correctional worker, Hickey took the major role in the initial staff contacts. As for the staff, we took the approach that the work of a correctional officer, given the right context, could have a positive meaning. All employees were invited to the introductory sessions. Most came to the meetings mainly to "get away from the women [the prisoners] for three hours." Hickey's introductory remarks were usually somewhat as follows:

> Let me explain why I am here. My first correctional experience was at the Training School for Boys. Somehow, I liked it and felt that it was a good place to be. It used to irritate and frustrate me to see staff who had all kinds of things to offer but weren't in a position to communicate their experience. . . . Anybody who makes it through six months in a correctional setting and gets banged around knows the art . . . yet it is never called a profession. . . . Because of the high turnover, you get the feeling that, hey, if I can last here, I must be doing something right. If you can deal with all the people around you, you must have special skills. Very few seem able to do it. Look at all the people who last only a few weeks or months and leave. The people outside are afraid of inmates. . . . This job is important, and that's why we are here . . . to try to give people a feeling that what they are doing is meaningful.

To interested employees, we offered to run advanced training workshops on moral development theory as a basis for changing prisons. We assured them that as outsiders we would have relatively little direct impact on the inmates. If there were to be dramatic results, we knew, the line officers would have to provide the major contact with inmates.

Fifteen self-selected correctional officers called "matrons" attended the training sessions, which dealt with problems and dilemmas introduced by them. In one session, for example, a correctional officer named Ellen discussed the question of whether or not it was right for a staff member to lie to inmates.

Ellen: I think you have a better relationship with the women when you are open and honest. You asked about an instance. Here is one. The women were picked from the institution to go to the Lakeville conference, and many women were interviewed. Two weeks ago, I had two women in the cottage come and ask me if I knew who was picked from the cottage, among the ones interviewed, to go to the conference. I knew nothing about it. Frankly, none of the staff in the cottage knew anything about this conference. We came in cold; it was just by inquiring that we found out what it was all about. So, about a week ago, we got a call that so and so in our cottage had been chosen to go to this conference. We were told not to let anyone know. "Don't let anyone know this woman is going. She knows herself, and we will be sending personal clothing to the cottage, but keep them in the closet. Ask her if she needs a sweater or a scarf, and we will get it for her, but don't release this information to the rest of the women."

Now, this is stupid. We know this girl is going to tell her friends, and the friends are going to tell others. Then someone said, "Do you know who has been chosen to go to the conference?" And you know what I said? "Yes, I do, but I am not at liberty to say at this time." But I should be able to say yes; it should be all in the open so that everyone knows what is going on.

Sue: But it all boils down to "Why lie?" Why not be open and aboveboard and say, "Yes, so-and-so has been chosen; you realize that the institution couldn't send all the women, and if you have any questions, go see so-and-so"?

Barbara: Why should we be put on the spot? If we were told facts and not put on the spot, we could better handle situations. When you are just in the dark and don't tell anybody, it is kind of foolish.

Sue: Everybody else is going to know anyway. By the time the inmates in the storehouse fill the clothing order or deliver the package, they are going to know that so-and-so is getting something special.

Ellen: And the one who has been chosen is going to go back and tell her friend, and her friend is going to tell so-and-so that she has been picked for this. What difference does it make? Lay it on the table and say, "This is it; so-and-so has been chosen for this reason." Wouldn't it be better, and a lot easier?

Joan: This is the thing: There is such a lack of communication between the correctional officers in the cottages and administration, in many respects. Why can't a little memo be sent out? We sometimes find out things from the women first, and we don't even know what it is all about; we have to stop and find out. To me, it would seem like we are working with the women; we are directly involved with them. We are the ones who have the most contact with them because we are right in the cottages.

One recurrent complaint was the lack of autonomy of the cottage officers who were given little discretion in decision making, even in such trivial matters as whether or not to allow a group of inmates to play volleyball. The correctional officer's job was seen as being essentially that of a custodian concerned largely with security checks and locking doors. Since the disturbance, relationships had deteriorated to the point that inmates openly taunted the officers, so it was nearly impossible for officers to feel they were respected by the inmates or providing any useful services.

In addition, correctional officers were repeatedly placed in a number of structural binds. For example, they were required to enforce a twenty-three-page rule book with instructions such as "If a woman shall have more than four pieces of toast, then she shall lose her toast for three weeks, during which period if another woman shall give her a piece of toast, that woman will lose her toast privileges for two weeks." Needless to say, these rules were difficult to enforce. Moreover, in order to control the cottages to any degree, officers had to make accommodations with powerful inmates, which meant overlooking certain rules and procedures. But when things went wrong, which they often did, correctional officers would be "brought up" by administration for not sticking to the rules. Officers often felt that administrators did this largely to cover up for their own incompetence. Thus, working with the line staff, we tried to develop a plan for a cottage unit that would correct some of their grievances yet work within our theoretical premises. With York's approval, we developed an experimental or model cottage, to be opened in the fall of 1971, in a twenty-two-room residence and that would differ from the existing cottages in a number of ways. First, it would be run semiautonomously, independent of administrative restriction, in order to give the staff greater latitude in negotiating with the inmates and to make them feel a new sense of importance in their roles. This step was particularly necessary, we felt, because we believed our project required flexibility that could only be achieved by granting greater control at the unit level. Second, the correctional officer's role was to change from that of rule enforcer to that of democratic leader, working directly with inmates in counseling and community meetings. By having staff and inmates participate in democratic decision making, we hoped to generate a sense of mutual respect and give the officers' jobs new meaning.

Staff members were understandably apprehensive. As one said, "You've been talking about giving the girls a lot of freedom, and from what some of them say you are going to sit down and let them make the rules. The biggest problem is this homosexual thing. What if they say that's OK? What will you do?" In a series of painful discussions, we attempted to convince the officers that allowing joint participation in decision making was an opportunity to achieve greater trust between staff and inmates and that inmates, we hoped, would be aided in their moral maturity and helped in their postrelease adjustment. It soon became clear that, to get the staff and administrators to go along with our project, we had to be careful to limit the scope of our democracy. Thus, initially, we agreed to let democratic participation extend only to internal discipline within the cottage and to planning cottage recreation; decisions regarding phone calls, work release, and furloughs were to be retained by the administration. "This way," said one administrator, "we can be sure the inmates won't vote themselves out of jail."

In selecting six officers from a list of ten volunteers, we looked for highly flexible yet committed people who could work with a range of inmates in a variety of settings. We chose a diverse group, ranging in age from twenty-two to fifty-six and in education level from a tenth-grade education to a bachelor's degree in philosophy.

"Constitutional Convention" Meetings and the Cottage Constitution

The first definition of the program achieved, we began meeting with small groups of inmates. Initially, they assumed the worst; for instance, the first question asked was whether or not we were cops, and Hickey was accused of being an undercover state police narcotics agent. When we tried to explain our ideas for a model cottage and asked inmates whether they would be interested in planning new cottage rules in collaboration with staff, most told us they did not like to "talk with pigs," listed various staff atrocities, and attempted to convince us that the staff was laughing at us behind our backs. Finally, after a month of meetings, most of the inmates we spoke with agreed to at least show up for the first meetings with the officers. Amid this climate of general mistrust, we began our first "constitutional convention" meeting in August 1971, with the announced goal of framing a set of rules for a self-governing cottage.

Fifty-four of the eighty eligible inmates—"eligible" meant those inmates with at least five months of time remaining to be served on their sentences—appeared at the first convention meeting. Knowing it was critical that we establish ourselves as independent mediators between staff and inmates, we discussed our earlier training relationship with the officers and suggested to both groups that we would attempt to remain "objectively neutral" and fair in the disputes that everyone knew would occur. We offered our ideological lecture about justice and suggested that this philosophy might provide a mutually agreeable basis for the rules of the institution. In this spirit, we solicited ideas, criticisms, and suggestions regarding the rules of the future model cottage.

The following week, an inmate named Janet presented us with an impressive list of suggestions:

1. *Medication.* "Upon entering the institution, I think every drug addict (whether it's a pill popper, heroin addict, methadone user . . .) should be given the proper medication for at least four days and something to allow her to sleep."

2. *Graded Cottage System.* "I think there should be a type of system started where, after being on this farm for a while, a girl can decide herself where she would like to live. Not to be jumping from one cottage to another, but one permanent residence."

3. *Rules.* "First of all, you can't have maximum [security] rules in an institution that has a minimum [security] setup. The way this institution is set up at the present time, it is considered minimum, so why have all these maximum rules? And some of these petty rules have to be done away with."

4. *Language.* "You can't take a girl from a ghetto (where about 95 percent of us are from) and expect her to come directly up to

your standards of living. Granted, this is jail, and there are rules one has to abide by, but to try to bring a black (or white, even) girl who has been speaking this way all her life into jail and expect her, the same day, to come up to a white standard of living and speaking is impossible. In order to do so, one must be used to it, and believe me, I am not speaking for myself, it is gonna take more than six months—one year; two, even—to make a girl change her whole way of living, and her manner of speaking, as long as she is not used to yours. As long as she is not disrespecting the staff, this should be ignored when she is speaking to another girl."

5. *Attire.* "I think a girl should be allowed to wear her own clothing, if she wishes to do so. I mean, after all, women (most) like to keep their appearance up, and these state clothes don't do anything for anybody; I don't care how you try to fix them up, it's all in vain."

6. *Money.* "I don't see why a girl can't spend as much money as she wants; I mean, after all, it is hers to do with as she pleases. I can see you wanting a girl to save some, but that doesn't mean she can't spend the money she gets from home. If one can buy a stuffed animal, all should be able . . . if one can buy a radio, all should be able to. No one here is better than the next one, regardless of what house they are living in. So I think we should all be treated the same."

7. *Visiting.* "In some states, anyone can come and visit, as long as you put them on your list when you first enter the penitentiary. The rules for visiting should be changed, I think, because some girls don't even have no family, just friends, and I think they should be allowed to visit these girls. Another thing, some families are very close, as I feel mine is, and I am just as close to my cousin as I am to my brother. After all, cousin is just a name stuck on a relative, and as far as I am concerned, the 'label' doesn't exist. But I feel some of the visiting regulations should be changed, for the simple reason that one visit could mean a change for the better in a girl's whole attitude."

8. *Rehabilitation.* "Every institution such as this, where there are people doing big time, should have some other means of rehabilitating the girls other than group therapy and education. Because that is all this penitentiary has to offer. There should be more expressive things for the girls to do. And one should not have to be on a certain level to be allowed to participate. 'Learning is in doing,' and we should be doing more."

"These suggestions should be read by a level-headed, broad-minded person who does not have a hang-up about minorities or people on a lower level than themselves."

Both staff and inmates were impressed by Janet's proposals, and, in spite of the distrustful climate of the institution, in the weeks that followed we were deluged by inmate rule suggestions. A format was adopted in which rules proposed by an inmate were discussed in the inmate-staff meeting. If after (often bitter) negotiation both groups agreed on the rule, a joint proposal on it was submitted to York. If she contested the rule, it was discussed in a meeting between her and us (the authors).

In all these sessions, long-standing mistrust between inmates and staff surfaced again and again, as did a surprising gap in moral perspectives. For instance, in one meeting, in a debate about whether there should be a rule against stealing all property or just inmate property, inmates stated in Stage 2 terms they would rip off institutional property with few qualms, whereas officers argued in Stage 4 terms that all stealing was "absolutely wrong."

Carol:	I feel stealing (from another inmate) is a very awful and foul thing. That's about the worst thing I think somebody can do to you, and I think punishment on that should be worse.
Adams (staff):	How about stealing from the institution and not from another woman?
Sal:	Good for them!
Smith (staff):	I guess it's how the individual feels.
Adams:	Isn't stealing wrong no matter who it is from?
Sal:	The State of Connecticut is rich and the taxpayers are paying for it, so why not steal when you are at work?
Ann:	A couple of gallons of ice cream was stolen out of the kitchen. Do you really think the girls stole it? The staff takes a lot of stuff out of the kitchen.
Smith:	The girls stole it. It was found in their room.
Ann:	If we got some decent food, we wouldn't have to steal from central kitchen.
Elizabeth:	[We] take ballpoint pens.

Lydia:	If you [the administration] would issue them, we wouldn't have to steal them. We have to beg for pencils!
Ann:	We could have our own pens, and they would tell us they were theirs. We have to beg for pencils, so why don't you start issuing pens and pencils?
Joan:	I would never steal from another inmate because we are all up here in the same position, and all of us, as far as money is concerned, it is pretty tight, you know? And I feel the state has taken a whole lot from me, and I don't feel as bad about taking from the state as from another woman up here.
Adams:	But, any way you look at it, stealing is stealing.
Jones (staff):	I feel the same way. This is theft, and theft is theft.

Because an estimated 80 percent of the Niantic population participated in some form of homosexual act during their incarceration, the most heated debates involved the issue of homosexuality. One inmate stated that she saw no cause why anyone should be locked (up), even for a sexual act, "because sex is going to be sex . . . I feel it should not be knocked until tried." The staff expressed shock at the language and the often not-so-veiled sexual invitations, but the inmates countered that any activity one might desire to engage in that might be offensive to other people should be done discreetly. This proposal seemed reasonable to many inmates, but it offended the staff's sense of institutional propriety. One staff member responded, "You have it better here than you do on the outside. I've still got to go to work. Remember, this is still a jail."

For years, the institution had refused officially to admit that a "homosexuality problem" even existed. One senior administrator insisted, "We don't have a homosexual problem here at Niantic, just a lot of immaturity." Interestingly, there was not even an official rule against homosexual activity. Instead, there was a plethora of rules covering public homosexuality without ever confronting it openly. For instance, holding hands wearing pajamas downstairs, sitting on floors, sitting with another person on a chair, and leaning against bedroom doors were all forbidden. Correctional officers had the uncomfortable task of preventing affairs between the women by such devices as separating homosexual couples, watching to see that couples did not sneak off to one of the rooms, and stalking after inmate couples.

After many discussions about the morality of homosexuality, a senior administrator finally said, "Look, I don't care any more whether homosexuality is right or wrong. This cottage has to have a rule at least saying that homosexuality is not allowed. Otherwise, two weeks after the cottage opens, some politician will ride down here with his black car with American flags on both fenders and close the place and get himself a good article in the newspaper."

The inmates understood the potential political issue for the institution and recognized there were serious moral problems when an unwilling partner was involved, where the personal sensitivities of residents and staff were violated, or when the unity of the entire community was in jeopardy. They finally conceded they could accept a rule restricting homosexuality, provided it was realistic. Some of the correctional officers also acknowledged that if homosexuality was the inmates' preference its practice should be recognized—particularly in view of the fact that recent state legislation had decriminalized homosexuality between consenting adults. They agreed not to engage in the largely unsuccessful witch hunts to attempt to enforce the largely unenforceable rules governing sexuality. Thus, through this rather slow process of negotiation there developed a working arrangement that lasted, although slightly modified, for six years.

Compromise was also achieved in other conflict areas. In early proposals, inmates asked for privileges such as color television sets, which the staff regarded as "pure rip-offs." However, after long negotiations, the proposals were modified to include requests most officers would accept, such as permission for inmates to wear their own clothing instead of the state-issued jeans and sweatshirts, the right to visit each other's rooms at will, increased freedom of movement within the cottage, and a democratic voice in disciplinary decision making—all substantial gains. Even the practice of locking inmates in their rooms at night (so that they were forced to relieve themselves in chamber pots) was done away with through negotiation. The final proposals were characterized by a certain moderation quite different from the earlier, more hostile proposals.

This long process of negotiation finally resulted, in September 1971, in the model cottage constitution, a document that, although not enthusiastically received by all, was at least acceptable to most. The preamble read as follows:

> We, the women of the Model Unit, hope to become responsible adults by developing self-confidence, self-respect, self-discipline, and honesty through collective thinking and organized efforts.
>
> Having attempted in some way to fulfill some of these personal and group objectives by shared feelings and thoughts, we will become more understanding, considerate, and trusting of each other.
>
> We hope to use the knowledge of our past experiences as a stepping stone for dealing with present realities and for a more meaningful future.
>
> We feel by putting this knowledge and wisdom to use we will be able to demonstrate responsibility every day of our lives. With this same knowledge, we hope to obtain courage to face everyday living in a rational way.
>
> Through all these goals, we hope to achieve identity and return to society not only as receivers but as contributors.

The preamble was followed by twenty-three "final general" rules, the first seven of which read as follows:

1. If a woman is sick or not feeling well, she should notify the medical department. If the medical unit says she must be admitted, the woman must do [as told]. Otherwise, the woman may return to the cottage to rest and not be locked [in her room].
2. Women should not be required to go for meals if not desired, nor should they be locked, but allowed to continue whatever [they were] engaged in, reading, watching TV, and so on.
3. Women should not have to be locked in their rooms at night; being belled in is sufficient.
4. Women should be allowed to smoke in the dining room.
5. We feel in working toward responsibility [that] the bedtime hour should be set at 11:00. If there is enough staff coverage, a later hour should be considered, and lights [should be allowed to] remain on until it is requested to turn them off [by the women]. Normally, women will be in their rooms at 11:00.
6. The house should have its own recreation committee to plan house functions for weekends and holidays.

7. Day work should be a cottage staffing decision made by cottage
   staff.

Accompanying these gradual accommodations was a change
in attitude in the meetings. Correctional officers would note privately
that Inmate X "wasn't that crazy." Inmates would admit that Officer
Y "wasn't that much of a pig after you got to know her." Either the
two groups had decided to cooperate out of sheer fatigue, or they had
begun to believe that there was a possible alternative to destroying
one another.

In the last meetings before the opening of the model cottage,
many inmates eliminated themselves from consideration as participants in the cottage. Of the forty inmates who attended our first
meeting, fifteen dropped out immediately because they were being
released within a month or so, and an additional thirteen withdrew
for various reasons. Some did not want to leave friends in traditional
cottages, some said they were "afraid of groups," some did not like
"others who might be in the model cottage," and some simply did not
like us, the authors. The unit opened with seventeen inmates and six
staff.

Problem-solving meetings were conducted weekly during July
and August 1971. By late August, staff and inmates were able to
jointly discuss the rules and the model cottage constitution so that by
October 1 the unit was ready to open. And open it did! Within an hour
after the inmates had moved into their new home, state police
informed prison officials that a six-year-old boy from the town was
missing and feared drowned in the prison's lake. Immediately, Deputy Commissioner York instructed that honor women and the model
cottage prisoners could join in the search. The entire cottage was
vacated as prisoners tramped the woodland surrounding the lake,
calling for the little boy. Twenty minutes later, we were told the boy
had been found by a neighbor. All we could do was await the return of
the prisoners. Since nearly all the model cottage inmates were considered hard-core problems and many had been participants in the May
uprising and because the search was totally unsupervised, we began
to get the sinking feeling that the intervention might well be doomed
before it got started. Gradually, however, first one inmate and then
another emerged from the brush, and within a short time all the

women had returned. The remainder of the day was filled with laughter and good-natured kidding as the inmates and staff told of their adventures during the search. Of course, looking for lost children does not happen every day.

The Operations of the Model Cottage

When the model cottage opened, staff and inmates quickly discovered that a serious commitment was required to maintain the cottage constitution and to respect the cottage structure as valid in itself. Initially, inmates found it difficult to cooperate with the "police" or to put themselves in a position of having to punish one another for breaking a rule. However, during the cottage's second week, an incident occurred that showed such an idea was possible.

An inmate named "Big Debby" appointed herself house manager, and she threatened to "stomp" anyone who did not follow her orders and "clean up their shit." After a day of her calling everyone epithets, several women decided it was time to call a house meeting on Big Debby herself. Debby marched into the meeting, announced she had brought her "stomp boot to group," and said she would slug anyone who brought her name up. After a long while, a highly respected inmate who had done a great deal of prison time declared she was "fed up with Big Debby's horseshit." Another inmate, who had previously said she would do anything but lock up her sisters, added that for the respect of the house and everybody in it "something would have to be done about Debby." Yet another inmate said, "Debby has gone too far." All seventeen inmates in the room affirmed that Debby could not be allowed to go about the model cottage cursing and threatening everybody, and by majority vote it was decided Debby would be locked in her room for a day. The group also prohibited her from future cursing and threatening. In response, Debby threatened to leave the program and went to her room to pack her bags. Minutes later, however, she had more or less accepted her discipline sentence. From then on, the principle that the inmates were going to handle their own was firmly established in the life of the cottage.

In order for the Just Community cottage to work, staff and inmates had to accept two core cottage institutions—the community meetings and the small groups. The focal point of the program was the community meeting, which could be called by an inmate or staff member at any time. When a cottage rule offense was discovered, the people at the community meeting acted as a jury, determining guilt or innocence. If discipline was required, it was determined by a discipline board made up of two inmates and a staff member chosen at random. Matters such as work assignments and interpersonal conflict were dealt with through open discussion. Occasionally the community meeting dealt with issues of contraband, assault, and attempted escape. Every ten weeks, a marathon meeting was held in which cottage rules were redefined, and there were often further negotiations with administrators as to the types of issues the cottage could deal with. It should be emphasized that rules and disciplinary procedures applied equally to staff as well as inmates.

An example of cottage decision making in the community meeting format may be seen in the case of an inmate named Jerri, who had assaulted another inmate named Rose. Earlier in the week, the group had expelled an inmate named Betty for a similar assault under similar circumstances. Both Betty and Jerri had had repeated histories of violent behavior, in and out of prison. In Jerri's case, however, the dilemma posed to the group was that an hour before the assault Jerri had approached Jones, a staff member, and *asked* to be locked in her room because she "felt anger building up" and was "afraid of what she might do to Rose," who had rejected her homosexual advances. Jones had refused to lock up Jerri, saying that she should be able to deal with her emotions. The group debated whether Jerri should be expelled from the cottage, as Betty had been earlier in the week.

Burns (staff):   What about Jerri? Should she leave?

Barbara: All I know is Jerri tried to beat Rose. Then she should leave, too.

Jean: Yeah, it's physical violence.

Smith (staff): If you are going to be fair, don't we have to deal with the thing on a group basis? Look, we have a rule in the constitution on violence.

Jessica: But Jerri asked Jones to put her in the infirmary and give her medication. She told you what would happen.

Sue: I see that, but does that excuse what she did to Rose? I don't know. It's hard. I see that we should be flexible about it. If she told the staff, then that puts the weight more on the staff than on her.

Debby: But still, Jerri can't go around pulling on people's hair and knocking them down. She should go, too. How can you kick Betty out and talk this shit about Jerri? It's the rule.

Joan: In society, doesn't being crazy kind of excuse you? Like they put crazies in Norwich [mental hospital] . . . not here in Niantic.

Sue: I don't know what we are going to do with you, Jerri. I see what you are saying about telling staff when it's too much for you to handle, but still there's the thing of fairness with Betty.

Bobbette: Is there something else we can give her? You know, that she would feel as bad as if she left, like lock-up? That might help her to think.

Jackie: But lock-up don't do nothing for you. Just gets you crazier.

It was finally decided to allow Jerri to remain in the cottage under strict supervision and loss of all privileges for a period of one month, which was a greater loss in terms of personal comfort than being expelled. The unit felt that somehow her case was different from Betty's, since Jerri had informed the staff members of the impending violence.

We sought with the community meetings to establish the "community ideal" as a new moral referent group. It was hoped that both staff and inmates would increasingly judge their actions in relation to the moral consensus of the cottage community. To accomplish this, when leading the group we attempted to point out contradictions between an individual's moral statements and her actions. For example, a staff member was reprimanded in one meeting for "not showing concern in doing her job." Similarly, an inmate was reprimanded by the group for not reporting an escape because this showed she "didn't care enough for the people in the house." We saw such disciplining as a means of establishing group norms rather

than primarily as a deterrent to bad behavior. Slowly staff members
sought to pose ethical issues relevant to the case at hand. The early
meetings were long; some lasted as long as eight hours as all participants mastered the skills necessary for self-government. Punishments
were generally mild and erratic during this period as well. This was
due largely to the lack of skill in self-government and group leadership on the part of both staff and inmates. Other forces were at work,
however, that were not easily discernible yet played a central role in
shaping the community. First, inmates in general are ever mindful of
their need to "look good" for the parole board. Typically, this means
working on some personal weakness that might help convince the
paroling authorities of one's reformation. An addict, for example,
might join a self-help group or attend therapy of some kind. Thus, at
Niantic, while the issue of fairness within the unit was paramount in
our minds, it was not always the chief concern for the prisoners.
Disciplinary issues gradually came to serve two functions. They
supported the group norms established by the community while
simultaneously providing a treatment mechanism useful for parole.
This was accomplished by a discipline mechanism referred to as
"contracts" by the community tailored to individual shortcomings.
For example, an inmate with a particularly violent temper, involved
in a fight, might be punished by the community in addition to the
more traditional sanctions by requiring that she curb her outbursts
for a specified time. The danger in this practice, of course, was that
the unit's home rule, and ultimately the entire program's, might lose
its moral force with respect to the community's welfare in favor of
personal self-interest. Many community meetings were devoted to
this issue.

A second force that had a profound impact on the community's development was the issue of staff discipline. In theory, the model
unit was a democratic self-governing enterprise dedicated primarily
to justice as an end in itself. Certain realities, however, precluded full
implementation in this area. First, there were the obvious inequities
implied by virtue of the fact that staff did not live in the units full time
nor could they be sure that they would always work in the unit given
the chronic manpower shortage that constantly plagued the prison
staff. The net effect was to necessitate a double standard of conduct.
Thus, a grievance with a staff member might be postponed several

days pending her return, which often tended to defuse the issue. Second, and more profound, however, were the obvious inequities surrounding the relative power position of inmates and staff. The various reforms accomplished by the Just Community program in the model unit were in no sense guaranteed. They were privileges that could be revoked at the will of the staff. There was no way, therefore, that staff and inmates could ever be subjected to exactly the same standard of justice. This was reflected, primarily, in the reluctance of the unit to confront staff transgressions with much enthusiasm. Nevertheless, the fact that the unit did achieve a high degree of self-government in spite of these built-in constraints is a tribute to the personal integrity and professionalism of the staff.

Besides the community meetings, inmates and staff participated every week in three small group meetings. These groups operated much like peer-counseling groups in traditional therapeutic communities, but with two important differences. First, there was a conscious avoidance of "medical-model" language; the groups were designed to solve problems, not cure hang-ups. Second, there was an effort to let the inmates rather than staff act as the primary therapists. Inmates were encouraged to offer other inmates insights, as much to train them in listening and empathizing as to give recipients good advice.

Neither community meetings nor small groups were easily established. The staff members initially objected to inmate "gaming" (game playing) in community meetings as vociferously as inmates objected to disciplining other inmates. Staff members also found it difficult to handle their conflicting obligations toward community and institution. For example, when a rumor spread through the administration building that the model cottage was dealing with a "spike incident" (incident involving a narcotics needle) and the superintendent called about the matter, she was told by a line officer that she was sworn not to betray the cottage's confidentiality rule. To the credit of both superintendent and officer, the incident was worked out amicably, but the dilemma clearly pointed up the conflict in allegiance between institution and cottage.

Small groups also required much of the participants. Staff members had to learn to be genuinely nonjudgmental when listening to inmate concerns. Such nonjudgmental counseling was nearly impossible at first when inmates outspokenly stated that they "really liked to shoot dope" or "do prostitution." Inmates often found it difficult to open up in the small groups, fearing their confidences might end up in a parole file or that other inmates would not honor the group's confidentiality and would "spread their shit up and down the road."

During the first year of the program, there was a 50 percent turnover in staff participating in the cottages. Two of the original six decided they did not believe in the program, saying it let the inmates "get away with murder." Another staff member quit, saying simply that she was "burned out." These incidents revealed to us the importance of matching staff to the program goals. They also strongly suggested that a staff member being paid less than $10,000 a year (in 1971), with little real hope of advancement, could not be expected to sit through five or six 4-hour groups per week for an indefinite period of time without official recognition or compensation.

The first year of the program was perhaps its most difficult year, but it also may have been its most successful. The participating inmates were all veterans of the days of the riot, of the "constitutional convention" meetings, and of the birth pangs of the program, and so they thoroughly understood the program's goals and political rationale. Later inmates would speak almost reverently about "the first women and how they had changed all those foolish rules," and, indeed, many of the first inmate participants were leaders rather than followers. Not one of these first-year graduates is now in prison; three are now directors of rehabilitation projects of their own, and the others are leading productive lives as mothers, workers, and students.

But a successful democratic justice program in prison is not just a successful first year. A meaningful reform program must maintain itself and adapt to new conditions. During the first year at Niantic, critics pointed out two major omissions in our work. Progressive penologists observed that we had done little to prepare graduates of the Just Community model cottage for a return to society. Conservative critics, including some in the correctional bureaucracy, wondered if our program would work with a male population. Let us examine our experiments in response to these two criticisms.

The Just Community Halfway House

In the spring of 1973, Hickey was assigned by Connecticut corrections commissioner Manson to investigate the possibility of creating alternative community correctional centers that would be cheaper and more beneficial than housing women at Niantic. We decided to use the Just Community format, as in the model cottage at Niantic, in a halfway house located at the New Haven YWCA, which was in the center of the city's drug culture and offered all of the temptations of inner-city urban life.

In April 1973, halfway house inmates, who were former Niantic inmates, began to propose and consider rules that would follow those of the Niantic project but would allow residents greater freedom, consistent with the realities of life in society. Creating such rules was a major task and was accomplished with far greater ambivalence than at Niantic. The rules had to allow the staff to account for inmates at all times, yet allow the inmates the freedom to encounter the terrors and pleasures of the streets. Several inmates observed that it was harder to be half-free than not free at all. The administration also put pressure on the model unit to create rules that would, in the superintendent's words, "ensure the program's success." The twenty rules that were finally developed in August 1973 reflected painful negotiation and earnest efforts to balance the contradictory goals of maximizing freedom while ensuring a viable program:

1. All women must have rooms in orderly fashion before leaving for jobs or school activities.
2. House meetings and groups precede any scheduled activity or unscheduled activity, with exception of work and school.
3. Automatic house discipline if someone on free time does not return by curfew.
4. Women must sign in and out, at all times—on the way to work, school, or anywhere.
5. Anyone found with alcoholic beverages or drugs in her possession, externally or internally, will be automatically sent home to the Farm [Niantic].

6. Anyone leaving house meeting has five minutes to return, or discipline will be in order.
7. Any woman has the right to appeal after half of her discipline has been served.
8. Contracts can be appealed at the next community meeting.
9. If after a twenty-four-hour period, a person still feels that her discipline is unjust, she may ask the discipline committee to reconsider the discipline. At this time, the committee may revise, change, or lift said discipline.
10. When on free time (recreation time), a woman must verbally give staff a report on the destination desired and the telephone number (if possible). Staff may check on resident's whereabouts, and a woman must call and report every hour when out on free time.
11. All procedures and regulations for YWCA residents must be followed.
12. No violence inside or outside the YWCA unit.
13. All women will be checked on periodically whether they have jobs, are at a training center, or are in school.
14. All money received on streets has to be turned in to the director.
15. Everyone is allowed $12.00 a week for spending money. This is obtained from the state.
16. You have to have a urinalysis after every furlough [to check that inmates were not using drugs]. There will also be a spot-check urinalysis.
17. Everyone should fill out their applications for jobs truthfully. (Tell them you're a convict.)
18. All incoming packages are to be checked, including items brought in from furloughs.
19. There will be no use of public transportation for furloughs except when traveling with the persons you have been furloughed to.
20. An outsider can go on the weekly activity if it is brought to the group beforehand and the group agrees.

The halfway house opened to great fanfare in the local press, with inmates and six staff members participating. Roughly a month after the doors opened, however, serious questions arose. Inmates Sue, Mary, Joan, and Betty were supposed to leave every morning at 8:15 A.M., and arrive at the restaurant where they worked at 8:40.

Instead, they would borrow the car of Sue's ex-pimp, drive to Bridgeport, buy some cocaine, and somehow manage to arrive at work only ten minutes late (despite a trip of thirty-eight miles). When the director of the halfway program, a former Niantic employee, became aware of the adventures, a community meeting was called. Sue was accused by the three others because she had actually been caught possessing drugs. Although Sue steadfastly refused to snitch on the same inmates who had just voted her out of the program, she became enraged and temporarily undone, tried to slash her wrists, and plunged through a closed window. Three hours later, a security officer arrived to return her to Niantic.

With this terrifying evening, the staff realized that the well-behaved inmates of Niantic hardly resembled the women who were now back in their community—and filled with the same passions and energy that had brought them to prison in the first place. They realized that the drug-involved inmates could not easily put aside their desires for cocaine, marijuana, or heroin and that the seemingly simple idea of detecting narcotics use through the urinalysis was not only far from being accurate but also tended to break down trust between inmates and staff.

In addition, the sense of community developed at the Niantic model cottage tended to disintegrate in the halfway house as inmates found themselves divided between their work, school, and program lives. For example, community meetings rarely included all inmates. As jobs were scarce, there was usually at least one inmate who had to work at night, thus making it impossible for her to attend community meetings. Moreover, the community setting made inmates hesitant to report other inmates for offenses, especially drug-related ones, fearing harassment or reprisals from other inmates or street friends.

No doubt, another avoidable difficulty lay in the employment of ex-inmates as staff aides or counselors. Although it was always tempting to hire program graduates, both to give them employment and to give inexperienced staff aid in understanding the inmate point of view, there were some negative consequences. One ex-offender counselor had to be removed for stealing, another shot heroin frequently with other inmates, a third pointed a loaded pistol at the director when he attempted to discharge her.

Finally, there was a gradual split between the Niantic and the New Haven projects. Part of this resulted from the personalities of the directors of the two programs. More important, there was a growing gulf between the community staff, who saw themselves as living in the real world, and the Niantic staff, who were comfortable in their own secure if "less relevant" environment.

After a stormy year, in which the New Haven program came close to dissolving at several points, a format was established that *began* to realistically cope with the complexities of the street-life dilemmas confronted by the women. For the community halfway house to succeed, it was clear the staff had to gain the trust of the inmates and encourage them to share their experiences, so that the groups could deal with them in terms of the just community model. This required a sense of community even stronger than that needed in the Niantic setting. The staff had to learn to be more willing to share their experiences with others.

The change in the community center model may be seen in the following incident. A urinalysis of two inmates, returning from a four-hour furlough, produced results indicating recent use of heroin. At a weekly community meeting, the director asked all the women present if they felt the program could tolerate inmates openly using drugs. The response was a resounding no. The director then offered to allow them to propose a discipline for the two women, without the staff present. The inmates met and suggested a harsh discipline— thirty days restriction to the halfway house—for the two women. The staff met separately and proposed a slightly milder penalty. When the staff and inmate groups reconvened, a compromise discipline was negotiated. This separate caucusing allowed inmates to consider the consequences of drugs in their own terms, permitted a more powerful indigenous inmate leadership to develop, and gave inmates a sense of ownership about the final decision, which was often not attained in the more protective prison program.

It was evident the tension of the street life with all its temptations required a more solid inmate culture as well as greater trust of staff than was needed in the prison-based program. This openness was successfully encouraged by the personality of the third and most successful director of the program. He was a young college graduate who had worked in the program from just after its inception. Often he led discussions on such topics as "What gives you the biggest high—a shot in the arm, playing with your baby, or making love?" Typically, inmates would respond by narrating vividly the kinds of experiences they encountered in their street and work experiences, while at the same time they were freed of the personal confrontativeness that characterized the prison meetings. This helped the staff to establish closer relationships with the individual inmates and develop more meaningful discussions about their experiences. Often there would be candid questions raised about what a life of crime meant to inmates; for instance, a check forger was asked if she would rather "make $500 a week cashing forged checks, with all the fear of the police, or $150 a week with no hassles?" The reality of such dilemmas far surpassed in power the more ethereal "What you gonna do when you get out?" discussions often heard at Niantic.

If there is a lesson to be learned from the short history of the New Haven community program, it is that democracy is probably far more difficult to achieve in an open setting but, in the end, probably has more potential for rehabilitation and education. The community feeling so successfully achieved in the Niantic program was, in part, a response to an artificial prison world where inmates were forced to live and share with one another. In New Haven, by contrast, this sense of community was far more difficult to achieve. Yet where there was fostered even a partial sense of purpose and interdependence that was based on the realities of inmate lives and not on the forced community of the prison, we could envision accomplishing the goals of purposeful reintegration. To paraphrase John Dewey, "The task of the school or prison must be about life." In this sense, the community program represented a vital step forward.

Bringing Men into the Just Community Program

The second major expansion of the program was initiated in 1974 when men were brought into the program for the first time. It had long been assumed that female prisoners differed in ideology and behavior from male prisoners, but there had been no reported effort to place men and women in identical program and architectural environments. We hoped our experiments would demonstrate that the

Just Community program could be effective with male as well as female inmates.

The literature on sex differences between male and female offenders gave us some insights as to the contrasts we might expect. In early studies on female prisoners (such as Ward and Kassebaum, 1960), striking differences were apparent between male and female responses to imprisonment. Although female prisons shared with male institutions a sharp polarization between inmate and staff worlds, it was suggested that female inmates enjoyed among themselves supportive relationships rarely found among male prisoners. Female inmates tended to evolve complex familial systems based on homosexual relationships.

The application of such findings to prisons must be made cautiously, since women's and men's prisons differ strikingly in several respects. First, women's prisons are typically different from men's institutions in structural design. Whereas men are characteristically housed in large (200- or 300-person) cell blocks, with little common living or social space, except for possibly a dayroom, women's prisons often house inmates in small household-size (20-person) cottages. Also, prison administrators' attitudes toward male prisoners differ quite dramatically from those toward female inmates: Male offenders are commonly perceived as "dangerous," whereas female offenders are most commonly perceived as "fallen." This attitude holds true even though a significant number of female inmates are incarcerated for violent crimes such as murder. The male prisoner is commonly "fought," "jammed," or "confronted" by the staff. The female prisoner is "directed," "protected from herself," or "helped." These differences—in space allotment and approach—undoubtedly affect the ways male and female inmates respond to imprisonment and the types of inmate communities that develop.

One of the best empirical works describing the differences between male and female prisons is that of Giallombardo's *Society of Women* (1966). Giallombardo observes that the prison provides the sociologist with a unique social laboratory with which to test cultural definitions of male and female roles. She suggests quite persuasively that men and women in American society, when confronted with imprisonment, experience different pains and losses. While a man most frequently faces the loss of his assertive and economic roles, a woman more commonly grieves for the loss of her maternal or sexual identity. Like Sykes (1958), Giallombardo argues that the inmate subculture in the prison represents a means of alleviating the deprivations of imprisonment. Faced with different role losses, the male inmate develops a radically different subculture from that developed by the female inmate. While the male in the traditional prison underworld seeks to retain something of his ability to "deal," "manipulate," "attack," or "resist," the female prisoner more commonly seeks to maintain her sense of attachment by identifying with an "intimate family," as well as seeks to keep intact her sexual attractiveness. Giallombardo suggests that, while the male prison subculture is marked by violent exchanges among inmates, the female inmate world is frequently far more supportive. This support is primarily based on the bonds of homosexual relationships between individual women and the kinship structures that help maintain these prison sexual ties, including other inmates who actually fill the roles of children, cousins, uncles, aunts, and so forth.

Although we were aware of Giallombardo's research, we undoubtedly underestimated the problems of adapting the Just Community program at Niantic to male inmates.

In the fall of 1974, fourteen male prisoners between seventeen and twenty-two years of age were transferred under Hickey's supervision from the aged cell blocks of the Cheshire prison to the North Building unit at Niantic, which had been vacated shortly after enduring the riot of 1971. Built in the 1920s, the North Building had served as Connecticut's first female prison, complete with a "tiger cage" in a basement security area, and more recently as its maximum-security facility. It was viewed by the authorities as an excellent opportunity to experiment with coeducation in prison with minimum political risk because of its location in an isolated part of the prison complex nearly a mile from the administration area. This aspect was particularly important, because the Connecticut Department of Corrections wished to assess the advisability of a new coeducational prison proposed for the Cheshire facility. This factor was stressed with the news media, and public opinion seemed at least indifferent if not supportive. Custodial interests dictated that prisoners with a history of sexual crimes be excluded, as well as individuals with less than six months remaining to be served. Since Niantic was already limited in vocational and industrial training, it was decided by the department that the men would be bussed daily to a nearby defense plant where they would receive federally funded training. This arrangement, however, failed to materialize shortly after the program opened, necessitating placing the men in the already inadequate Niantic prison industries.

Another reason for the creation of the unit was to provide in-service training for correctional officers at both Cheshire and Niantic who would eventually staff the new living units planned for Cheshire. A federal grant was obtained to assist with this aspect. Hickey, as project director, reported directly to the commissioner of corrections and was responsible for the selection and supervision of a unit director who in turn managed a staff of six male and female officers.

Within a few weeks after the first men arrived, one had a fistfight with a male staff member. Another had his sentence modified by a well-meaning judge, returned to Niantic with accomplices a few days later, and held up the central security center at gunpoint. Ironically, the inmates' accounts were the only monies taken. These were, thankfully, isolated incidents, but they revealed the basic male combativeness.

In small groups, male inmates showed a certain distance between each other and between them and staff members. For example, the following notes by Scharf during a single week in December 1974 show that in the female groups there were many exchanges of feelings and attitudes toward both staff and other inmates, whereas the male groups dealt almost exclusively with cottage conflicts and tensions.

> *Men.* Dave was frustrated with Jay not following through on his request to go to Seaside. Jim asked Dave if he shouldn't formalize his request. Dave didn't want to. . . .
>
> Jim tried a dilemma concerning the right to break a rule, as if an inmate is right to break a rule when a guard gives OK. Mike and George said they wouldn't want the same treatment if they were in the hole under these circumstances.
>
> Willie came in off the wall saying he didn't have to attend two groups in the same day. Smitty asked for a meritorious furlough even though he didn't have enough time. Dave

ran a rap about the injustice of his various sentences, a year flat and two "2-to-5's".

The issue was visiting the women. Chris said it was handled unfairly. He and Willie said they were visiting openly. Some of the complaints were legitimate.

Women. Pat opened group by asking everyone in group how they felt. The group asked Merle to lead group to give her more self-confidence. Some of the group got into the question of homosexuality, and Joan asked me some direct questions about my feelings on it.

Ruth opened. Barbara asked how she felt about going to New Haven. She said she was afraid of the halfway house, but everyone gave her their support. She asked everyone in the group to tell how they felt about her.

Posie began by saying she felt I came on wrong that morning by the way I criticized her. She admitted she was feeling down, and that's why she came off the way she did. . . . We asked Melba how she was feeling. Group felt she was staying in her room too much.

Edie talked about the warrants she was facing. Women talked about preparing to go to New Haven.

In the female model cottage, women commonly held hands. When a female inmate received a setback in her life, other inmates consoled her while she cried. Such support was almost nonexistent in the male program. This implied the existence of a natural community base among the women, which had to be artificially created in the male unit.

Yet, while there was perhaps little emotional openness in the male unit, the men had a political consciousness strikingly absent among the women. In several periods throughout the history of the men's program, the men moved to politically question the moral justification of the program. For example, the male inmates characteristically became far more involved in the creation of cottage rules than did the women. The female inmates more or less passively accepted the limits of their democratic power. When the female staff members, for example, ruled that the inmates could not deal with a specific issue, the women tried to offer reasons for the staff to change their minds but rarely challenged the staff's right to impose the limit. Once, when a cottage supervisor decided quite arbitrarily that the staff would unilaterally enforce the "drug rule" for a month, the

female inmates offered reasons for her to relent but made little effort
to protest the decision.

Supervisor: So that's why, ladies, the staff are going to enforce the
                drug rule. You have not shown us sufficient responsi-
                bility to deal with this matter.
Penny: But if we are responsible for a month, will we get it
                back?
Supervisor: We'll see how you act.
Karen: But this program is supposed to make us concerned for
                one another, right? How is this teaching us to be just
                and fair and show responsibility?
Supervisor: We want you to do those things, but show your concern
                in little ways before you attempt something big.
Lois: Oh, Mrs. _____, I think we've been trying. Don't you,
                Joan?
Joan (staff): I do. But I think you ought to wait for this.

    In contrast, the men actively pressed their limits. For example,
when the central office decided, with similar arbitrariness, to impose
a rule of not readmitting program graduates who were returned to
prison while on parole, this occasioned a political protest on the part
of the cottage inmates:

Walt (staff): We decided to make the decision about Mike [a parole
                violator]. There wasn't time to involve you guys . . . a
                decision had to be made.
Bill: I know what happened. You and Hickey got in your
                office and decided you didn't want Charlie here. So you
                axed Mike to make it look right.
Walt: Bullshit.
Sal: This is a fucked-up democracy. You come and pull this
                martial law bullshit. It wasn't so fucking urgent. You
                could have brought it to community meeting, but you
                decided.
Scharf: Walt, would you let group decide the thing if they
                voted to let Mike and Vic back?

Walt: I don't think they can be objective. They have a vested interest in the thing.

Jeff: I think group should vote on the thing.

Bill: I think if Joe P. . . . violated [parole] you would bring him back. The staff is afraid of Vic.

Sal: What I think we ought to do is give the director [Hickey] an ultimatum. If he doesn't agree to let us settle this thing, then we call the program a totalitarian society. . . . If it's a matter of wills, let's see who is stronger.

Rod: Do you have an attitude?

Sal: The real issue is whether the director of the moral development program has the right to infringe on the democratic power of this meeting. If it's true, let's kill democracy. We'll vote democratically, staff to have dictatorial powers.

Bill: It won't work. Then they really will make all the decisions. . . .

This type of dialogue was common in the men's community meetings. Another indication of political awareness was that the men's cottage constitution was more than fifteen pages long, complete with appeal procedures and stated rights of inmates. Male leaders also seemed to be unusually able in coping with and predicting the behavior of the administration.

These male and female differences evolved into radically different interpretations of the Just Community ideal. Over time, we came to call these two variations the *communitarian* and *political* approaches of the program.

The communitarian (women's) program assumed a solidarity between inmates and staff. Staff members would appeal to inmates to be concerned about one another and the community. The moral rightness of the community was only rarely questioned. Much like other communitarian models, such as the Black Muslims, the leader's role was to consciously build solidarity within the group and to represent the best ideals of the group. The women's unit supervisor, a tough-minded, sensitive black woman, was able to model and initiate

a value system most of the inmates could and did accept. This group
consciousness formed the moral core of the women's program.

The political (men's) program, however, assumed the polarization of inmate and staff interests, cultures, and values. The staff
assumed that there existed a staff perspective and a conflicting inmate
perspective. As inmates came to argue their position against the staff,
a natural moral dialogue occurred. Whereas the assumption of the
communitarian program was that inmates would come to take on the
moral perspective of the abstract cottage community, the assumption
of the political model was that inmates would come to identify with,
argue, and transmit the perspective of the inmate collectivity in the
cottage, and that, in arguing this position with the staff, moral
change would occur.

We are by no means sure, however, that the communitarian
model is necessarily associated with a female community, nor the
political model necessarily with a male one. For instance, the cottage
supervisor of the women's program viewed the communitarian
model as a style that matched her own personality. Also, the objective
situation of the men indicated a more political approach. Being men
in a women's prison, they were natural targets for stereotypes and
prejudicial treatment. Thus, the differences between the men's and
women's programs were the compounding effect of sex, selection of
leadership, and task differences rather than simply the result of
women preferring more communitarian forms of society than do
men.

We are not willing to label either the communitarian or political model as the "true" Just Community program. In terms of educational effectiveness, we hope to be able to uncover the relative merits
of a communitarian program that binds inmates to the group and
those of a political program that offers little perceived community
but does offer intensive moral and political debate. This question
may tentatively be resolved by comparing the changes in moral
judgment in the two programs over a number of years.

The problem of justice is more difficult to assess. The type of
justice in the two groups differed qualitatively. The women's program offered a communitarian type of justice in which there was a
supposed consensus among group members. In contrast, the men's
program's decisions tended to be the formal justice of an adversarial

judicial system. The rights of offenders facing cottage discipline seemed to be given more weight in the men's program than in the women's program. But the punishment in the men's program tended to be far harsher and there was less obvious support than there was in the women's program.

The three Just Community programs provided us with a natural and complex laboratory with which to study justice in prison. This accomplishment was not achieved without personal cost to those involved in the program implementation. At least two marriages dissolved among the staff members during this period, and the fifteen-hour days might have had something to do with this. Of the seven original officers who staffed the female program, only two were still working in the cottage in 1974. Despite the changes, a core ideology was created during this period that endured even with the turnover in staff and inmates. In effect, a program culture had been created.

An ongoing prison program such as ours requires social institutions, customs, and practices that allow it to endure over time. In the next chapter, we describe the institutions of the program, the community meetings, marathons, and small groups. The perceived legitimacy and justice of these institutions provide the truest test of any social program.

5

Prison Democracy in Practice

To achieve prison justice, we realized the Just Community program required institutions that would command the respect of inmates and officers—stable, shared social mechanisms that would serve critical community functions. Thus, the program's first years were marked by an ongoing effort to legitimize three central institutions: community meetings, marathon meetings, and small groups. The most important institution was the community meeting. Here rules were maintained and enforced and community conflicts were resolved. The marathon meetings met every twelve weeks and provided a context for the community members to recommit themselves to the program's contract. Small groups sought to provide a safe context for inmates to counsel one another, anticipate release, and work through personal conflicts. Let us consider these three institutions.

Community Meetings

Community meetings were theoretically concerned with issues involving the model cottage as a whole. In practice, however, inmates brought up personal problems in community meetings, just as they did in small groups.

The rules regarding issues for community meetings were simple:

1. Everyone had to attend every community meeting.
2. There would be at least one meeting a week.
3. Anyone, inmate or staff member, could call a meeting at any time. (This was modified when, during one week, six meetings were called in the early morning hours.)
4. No outsider would be permitted in the group without the consensus of the group.
5. If a disciplinary measure was authorized, it would be determined after the meeting by a discipline board composed of two inmates and one staff member (inmates were chosen on a rotating basis).

The meetings began whenever someone in the cottage yelled out "Group!" Within five minutes, all inmates and staff had dropped whatever they were doing and had appeared in the prison cottage living room. The meetings tended to be long, the record being 12½ hours. In a single night, a number of meetings might be called consecutively.

The meetings were guided by the correctional officers, although not in any didactic sense, and by applying the moral development discussion strategy they gradually gained expertise in running these meetings. When a concrete problem was raised in the meeting, they would attempt to find a moral issue implicit in the conflict. For example, if there was a question as to who would clean up the laundry that day, officers might try to extract a moral question underlying it—an inmate might be asked, "Joanie, is it right for you to sit on your butt while Mary has been cleaning the 'hopper' closet every day since last month?"

As the officers became more comfortable with the moral development approach, they increasingly perceived themselves as facilitators of discussion rather than as advocates of a staff point of view. They became aware of differences in moral stages and would attempt to encourage interaction across adjacent moral stages. For example:

Vicki: It's only wrong to steal eggs from the Northside, 'cause you might get brought up in group behind it.
Smith (staff): What do you think about what Vicki is running [saying]?
Patti: I don't know about that, Vicki. Would you feel right if people were ripping off and there was no trust, or concern on this farm, even worse than it is?

In contrast to classroom moral education, the model cottage discussions worked with real (rather than "canned") dilemmas, issues emerging from within the cottage itself. Inmate control of the discussions was also emphasized, although often at the expense of clarity or, at times, coherence.

The issues discussed in community meetings varied widely. During one 45-day period, the men's program reported twenty-one meetings and the women's program thirty-one. The log entries revealed that 76 separate topics were discussed in the men's unit and 84 in the women's unit. Table 5 indicates the relative importance of the different topics of discussion. With the exception of the more frequent inmate-inmate conflicts handled in the women's unit, there were similar patterns observed in both programs. Discipline decisions provided the major focus in each program, followed by staff-inmate and inmate-inmate conflicts.

Table 5. Discussed Issues in Community Meetings.

	Male ($N = 14$)	Female ($N = 17$)
Rule violations	38	43
Inmate-staff conflict	10	7
Inmate-inmate conflict	11	14
Rule making	10	7
Other	7	13

The flavor of these different topics may be seen in the log notations of two typical and roughly parallel weeks from each of the two programs. The log of the women's program, which was kept by the correctional officers, read as follows:

2/9: Meeting was called by Roberts and Colby (staff members) because of missing food from the kitchen. Cottage was unable to determine who the thief was, but Sue accused Jane of being a crook after Jane admitted to receiving eggs from the central kitchen. Nothing was really accomplished.

2/19: Sue, Jane, Betty, and Kay all went to the industrial building without permission and for no legitimate reason. Since it was Betty's second offense (same thing—she went to the administration building last time), she was disciplined. A contract was made with the other women, which states Sue, Jane, and Kay are to ask permission to go *anywhere* outside the front door, even to bring in milk. This will be for two weeks. Sue was disciplined today for her rudeness with Ann, Janet, and whoever else was around.

2/23: The community meeting attempted to deal with Diane, Toni, Pepper, and Dot, who did not sit in the designated area in the movies. They felt, after about a two-hour lecture was given, disciplining was not necessary. I disagreed and thought at least a contract was in order. But I doubt they'll do it again.

2/24: Diane called the meeting on Monica. Apparently, Jane smacked some toast away from Monica in fun. Diane made a comment which set Monica off, and Monica went storming off to her room. Diane called a community meeting. Monica explained that she was just nervous awaiting parole. She was asked to conduct herself more civilly and to attempt to talk things out.

2/26: Pretty good community meeting tonight. We got some amendments for the constitution which clarify our policy for admitting new residents (and returnees). We also discussed Jane and why she didn't go to work today.

2/27: The meeting was called by Trunbull [staff member] on discovering Lucy [an inmate on education release] at McDonald's making a phone call. She also presented evidence that Mrs. Owens saw Lucy on a motorcycle, driving into McDonald's, and that the institution has received an anonymous phone call reporting that Lucy was seen on Bank Street. The women immediately discounted the evidence, except that presented by Trunbull. Lucy, of course, denied being on a motorcycle but did not deny going off school grounds.

After a rather tense time, some women, particularly Toni, spoke up in support of Mrs. Owens, saying that she does not lie. The group, in light of all the evidence presented, gradually changed their position. Lucy was given the option of submitting to the institution discipline committee or accepting the unit's decision that she should drop out of the education release program. Trunbull and I also stressed the credibility of the unit.

When a vote was taken, nine women voted to take her out of the program; the rest abstained from voting. Lucy was upset and stormed out of the room before the vote was taken, but she was informed of the final decision.

From the log for the men's program, which was kept by correctional officers:

10/27: Disciplines were given for slips reviewed by discipline committee—see discipline log.

Josh read his discipline listing [of] examples of times in his life when his curiosity could of or did get him in trouble. Very little discussion followed, and the house voted unanimously to accept the discipline. Pete then read his, discussing his place in the house and his relations with each individual in the house, and although some dissatisfaction was expressed (not enough detail, too one-sided) the house voted 17 for, 1 opposed, to accept the discipline as given.

Lefty was probed about his furlough and his present plans for release. He went hunting illegally during his furlough and took some heat "for not using his head"—it seems that he is basically confused about what he wants to do. He was told to work out the few possibilities open to him with his parole officer and to think more about how he's going to cope with life on the street.

Ralph [asked Jake] what was going on with his big attitude and his "fuck you" attitude. It came out that [Jake] seems overprotective of his feelings: He admitted that he was basically insecure, felt bad about being small and "cute." He feels many of his thoughts are abnormal and won't reveal them and couldn't believe that anyone was sincerely interested in him as a person. The group tried to get him to view himself from different angles, realize what choices he had in life, and to deal with himself instead of hiding from his own problems. [He] was advised to mull the whole situation over and to bring it up in small group.

10/28: Meeting to decide about having marathon tomorrow. Earl [and] Don are taking the GED [high school equivalency examination] and Phil promised his boss to help with a job (in prison industries) that his boss cannot handle alone. Apparently the institutional assignments have *not* been notified. Complaints about poor planning.

Proposal to postpone marathon: for—6, against—8. Marathon will be held tomorrow.

11/2: House meeting [on] the fact that Joe [staff] did not have control over the keys for about 15 minutes. There was a great deal of tension over this. The meeting discussed how the house felt toward Dave's holding a meeting against the [house's] wish to have a house meeting during scheduled recreation. After this was disposed of, the keys were discussed. The sense of this was that it was a practical joke that went too far. The house was made aware of how serious this was.

11/4: Long discussion on "limits of democracy." Ernie said program could give residents more "say" than they have now. Dave said "Frontstreet" [the Niantic administration] put "walls around program." Will be discussed further in marathon. Good meeting, with much discussion by many people.

Enforcing Cottage Rules

A primary function of the community meetings was the enforcement of cottage rules as defined in the 1971 constitutional convention. Every infraction was handled, from "Suzy not cleaning her cup" to "Rose hiding in the bushes" to "Mary attempting to escape" and "Ellen getting caught with smack [heroin] in her room."

The right to handle felony-level offenses was not won easily. During the first year, there was an accidental assault on a staff member when she tried to intervene in a fight between inmates. The superintendent referred the matter to the community meeting, thus setting a precedent for the resolution of such offenses. In such situations, confidentiality was a serious problem for officers. For instance, when the assaulted officer arrived at the infirmary to have her ribs x-rayed and was routinely asked to fill out an accident report (for insurance purposes), she replied that it might violate the confidentiality of the house. Other incidents, involving drugs and even attempted escape, were "kept within the house" by staff members, presenting some with legal as well as moral conflicts.

Eventually, a compromise was arrived at in which the unit supervisor would share with the superintendent the nature of an issue in the cottage, but in very general terms—for instance, "We are dealing with a drug problem." The administration in turn allowed the cottage full authority in assessing penalties. This policy would become quite controversial from time to time among both program participants and institutional personnel, who rightly feared its inherent dangers. The compromise, of course, was in fact a temporary concession of power on the part of Superintendent York, who had personally pledged support for the program. It was also a sign of her confidence in the unit supervisor and staff. It was fraught with risks and legally unsupportable by either party, because the inmates were in fact largely disenfranchised. In final analysis, the compromise was a unilaterally granted privilege that could be rescinded at will. Its viability and, indeed, the perceived legitimacy of the entire program rested largely in the degree of trust both sides held for each other.

Another issue involved the equity of punishment of inmates in the different prison cottages. Once one officer from another cottage asked, quite reasonably, why a woman from the Just Community cottage caught with a marijuana cigarette should only have to write an essay whereas one of her women would have six months added on to her sentence.

However, only rarely was the power of the community meeting challenged, and it usually occurred as a result of politically explosive offenses taking place outside the cottage—two temporary absences by so-called dangerous male inmates and an attempt by a woman to smuggle drugs into the prison. Such cases were handled by the institution discipline board. In nearly all other cases, however, the prison administrators allowed the community meetings to handle discipline matters.

Most offenses dealt with in community meetings were fairly prosaic. Petty offenses were usually punished by a reprimand ("Now, that's really a stupid thing to do") or by the offender being ordered to write an essay. For instance, when Jane referred to an older woman with an epithet, she was assigned to do an essay on how older people react to profanity. "I didn't really think how [the woman] would react to me calling her a bitchy motherfucker," she wrote, in part. "I realize that some people, especially those who haven't had the ghetto experience, are not used to those kinds of words." In the meeting at which Jane presented her essay, there was a rather interesting discussion about the reactions of people of different ethnic and class backgrounds to profanity. Isabel eventually made a contract with the cottage not to use such words around people who might be offended by them.

More serious infractions often would elicit sterner group disapproval, and this form of moral sanctioning was perhaps the most common and effective means of dealing with violations of cottage rules. The discussion of an instance in which an inmate named Midge broke the house rule on confidentiality illustrates how strong the moral pressure could be:

Sue: She don't give a damn; she's going to do what she wants.

Midge: I *am* concerned.

Bea: Are you concerned about yourself?

Midge: Yes, I'm concerned about myself.

Carlie: Midge, why do you think we sit here and say and do the things we do to you?

Midge: I don't know.

Carlie: It must be something. People like to listen to records and watch TV, without spending their time on you . . . we are giving up what we like to do to talk to you, and it's not just because it's for something to do, either.

Midge: I don't . . .

Carlie: Remember, you had the same problem before, how you react. Wasn't there something when you first came here? You had a problem. You didn't learn anything from what happened, you know. I am talking about here, where you were on the verge of having a nervous breakdown or something.

Midge: I couldn't talk to anybody then.

Carlie: Who in here do you feel you can talk to now?

Midge: I can talk to anybody in this group about certain things.

Sue: Certain things.

Midge: There is probably a couple of people I could talk to.

Bea: About things that matter to you, huh?

Dot: I want to ask you, Midge, why you really wanted to come over here. Why?

Carlie: Tell the group why.

Midge: I wanted to come because I wanted to be able to relate to people more, because maybe I would be able to express myself better.

Bea: Do you feel disappointed in the house? You said you wanted
             to come in the cottage and see how it was. . . . Do you feel
             like nothing is happening, like we are at a standstill? . . .
             Do you feel bored?

Midge: No.

Dot: She couldn't possibly [feel bored] because ever since we
             started she has been the one on the floor. Everything we had,
             Midge has been on the floor. It's always Midge—why did she
             do this, or Midge this or Midge that—and Midge's not the
             only one who got a problem.

It was assumed from the outset that Midge was guilty of
"talking outside the group," and the meeting represented more a way
of reemphasizing the norms of the community than of establishing
Midge's guilt or innocence. Throughout the meeting, the other
inmates invited Midge to reenter the moral community of the cottage
and they asked her repeatedly if she was sincere or if she was disappointed in the house—all invitations for her to admit her offense
against the house and rejoin the community. Still, even though she
had broken "house rule," she was not punished. Simply humiliating
her and calling her (and other inmates') attention to the rule were
deemed penalty enough.

Serious violations of cottage rules often involved punishment
as well as group disapproval. The actual penalties imposed by the
community meeting were assessed by a discipline board, although
appeals could be made to the community meeting, which had the
power to overturn or modify the board's decisions. The disciplines
assigned by the board tended to be imaginative. For example:

- For disrupting a meeting, Jean must lead every meeting for the
  next week
- For repeatedly playing the radio too loud, Bobbie must sing for her
  supper for the next three nights
- For being out of place, Mary loses recreation privileges for one
  week and must write an essay on responsibility
- For persistent use of abusive language, Barb is not to be spoken to
  by anyone in the unit for two days

- For asking another person to break a rule, Sue may not ask anyone for anything for two weeks (to be enforced by the unit members)
- For stealing, Carlie is to be locked up after work until morning for three days and must write a letter of apology to the individual she stole from

At other times, stronger measures, such as expulsion, were called for. From 1971 to 1976, of the nearly 200 women, roughly 20 were expelled—12 for violence, 6 for drug use, 1 for breaking the confidentiality rule, and 1 for "being a general nuisance."

For an inmate to vote expulsion of another inmate required tremendous courage, since such actions violated the inmate code of "Never rat out another inmate." This was especially true when it involved returning the offender to Cheshire. An incident in the men's cottage illustrates this problem. Sam came to Niantic with a reputation of being a con man and soon after he arrived was discovered by staff in a storeroom with one of the female inmates. The residents disciplined him by placing him under a month's house arrest, with the warning that further behavior would lead to his return to Cheshire. The fact that Sam was new to the program and that several residents admitted to similar behavior in the same storeroom and, indeed, argued rather convincingly that some staff knew about its recent illicit uses, saved him from immediate expulsion. A week later, however, he and a fellow inmate decided to shinny down a drain pipe at 1 A.M. and visit two women friends in another cottage. As they were leaving, another inmate discovered them and warned them that he would notify the staff and have the project director, Hickey, called at his home immediately if they left. The staff were informed, and the two were apprehended. On their return, the community locked the pair in their rooms pending a full hearing the next evening when all staff could be present.

The next day, the unit director and Hickey met with Superintendent York who agreed to allow the North Building cottage to deal with the matter, although according to both state law and the prison's understanding with the cottage, the incident could have been labeled an institutional escape and thus involved either felony charges or at least summary removal.

At the community meeting, the entire incident was discussed for six hours, leading to a vote favoring expulsion. After the meeting, there were many recriminations among both staff and inmates accusing others of "doing the Man's work." Indeed, the moral issues raised in the discussion were extremely difficult and forced us to reexamine our own assumptions that justice could ever be done in prisons as they exist; for example:

- Should individuals be punished for having normal sexual desires particularly where there was mutual consent?
- What law did they break? (None.)
- Isn't the prison encouraging homosexuality by forbidding heterosexuality?
- What's fair about sending our men back to a hell hole like Cheshire and leaving the women here without any punishment?
- Is the only reason they're being expelled because it is politically embarrassing?

Similar painful dilemmas were occasionally faced in the women's program, although fortunately the matter of having to decide to remove an inmate from the program was relatively rare. Most punishments were seen as opportunities for educating both offender and community. For example, when an older, alcoholic inmate, who was expelled for taking a drink while living in the program's community center, returned to Niantic, the community meeting sought to get her to understand her role and the roles of the other inmates involved in the incident.

Ella: You see, on my furlough I went to my daughter's house and she had this bottle on her TV. I don't know what it was, some Mexican stuff or something like that, and it didn't bother me because I had no problems then and I wasn't thinking of drinking. And then I had a very disappointing weekend, so at two o'clock—I was supposed to be back by six—so by two o'clock, I poured myself one because I wanted a drink, so I had it. So I called Trish [staff] at my daughter's house and told them that I took a drink and that I wanted to go to an AA meeting after, but then, see, that one drink. . . . I thought it didn't bother me. So the house gave me permission to go to the [bridal] shower, and they all had drinks at the shower. Karen [a fellow inmate] offered me a drink. They had all kinds of drinks, and I went two rounds; I just had them in order, you know. . . . I think it was like a compulsion in my system, you know; I wasn't thinking about my job or anything. So Monday at twelve o'clock I punched out and I got a little bottle of 59¢ Southern Comfort—I think it was a shot and a half or something—and then I felt like going out to a tavern and really getting drunk. And then I thought, "Well, I won't do that because they'll send me back to Niantic." So I said, "I'll go back to the house and tell them that I took that one drink and maybe they can deal with me."

Barry (staff):	But do you think it was fair of them to send you back?
Ella:	Yes, because I shouldn't drink.
Christine:	If anything, Karen should have told her, "No, don't have a drink." Not, "Go ahead and have a drink."
Ella:	At first, I did blame Karen because that was a dirty trick for her to do. Because I wasn't drinking; I was toasting with a glass of water and, you know, I really didn't intend to drink. But she said, "Oh, go ahead, have a drink; I won't tell." If she was really concerned about me, she never would have said that. She would have said, "Don't drink."
Smith (staff):	But you could have said no, couldn't you? So why should you blame Karen?
Christine:	She could have told her not to have one. She knows Ella would have to come back here.
Smith:	But we're concerned about Ella; we want her to get to the point where she can say "No, thank you" to a drink whether or not Karen says go ahead.

Collective Ownership and Moral Values

Each democratically enforced instance of discipline seemed to be not only a form of deterrence but also a way to rally the moral sentiments of the group, to offer members a means of showing their support of the cottage contract, and to clarify the community rules, as well as to rearticulate the moral principle at stake in the rules. Throughout, there was a conscious effort to make rule violations the context for discussions about broader social issues. For example, in the incident just related, Smith successfully rearticulated two values implicit in the program: (1) that the group had a commitment to commonly held ideals, and (2) that each had a responsibility to respect and support each other in maintaining those ideals.

The key psychological principle underlying punishment-oriented community meetings was that staff members encouraged the sense of *common ownership* of the group. It has been postulated by Lewin (1951) and others that with collective ownership participants show greater openness and also change their basic ideology through their participation in the group. From a developmental perspective, both Mead (1934) and Cooley (1912) suggest that a person's role taking the group's collective sentiment may lead to more social maturity. By taking part in a single community, then, individuals learn to understand the moral perspective of other groups as well. Over time, they increasingly begin to see things from the point of view of the community, and they act accordingly. Cooley and Mead suggest that this ability to internalize the conscience of the group permits members to identify and comprehend the perspective of other collectives with which they later come into contact—and so to develop what might be called a genuine morality.

In our examples of community meetings, this giving away of ownership of the group was accomplished with reasonable success. In the group involving Midge, for instance, it was clear that the group was the *inmates'* group and that Midge had violated a norm that the other inmates shared. Others sought to encourage Midge to recant and show more feeling for the group, as well as to restore the cottage norm of confidentiality. This was not the case with all discipline offenses. The expulsion decision involving Sam and his companion was based, as we have seen, more on political expedience than on moral consensus. Similar responses occurred with what were perceived by the inmates as victimless crimes, such as "hootch brewing." Such incidents often resulted in a rather strained standoff between inmates, who were convinced that they were being prevented from "doing what anyone should be able to do," and the officers, who were sworn to enforce the conventional order of the institution. The following dialogue, resulting when two inmates were found to have hidden whiskey in their rooms, is typical:

Davis (staff): Now, Jane, you know that it's wrong to have liquor in a penal institution. You can't have people drunk and still run a prison.

Smith (staff): I agree. It's a matter of the rules. You ladies should know this.

Carole: No offense, Mrs. Smith and Mrs. Davis, but I'm an inmate with a drinking problem. I've been deprived a long time. Give me a bottle of whiskey, and I'll drink it. No way me or anyone else in this room would do different.

Bobbie: She's right. We's all gonna do the same, and we ain't going to police those dumb enough to get themselves caught.

Such issues were handled initially by the staff in different ways. One was hypocrisy ("We know you're doing it, but don't let us catch you"); another was moralizing ("Pot smoking is bad; people who use it are breaking down their health").

A more promising approach was to get inmates engaged in a frank, discussion of the moral issues involved. For example, another incident, in which a male and female inmate were caught having sex. led to a debate about the institutional rule prohibiting sex. The men stated that most of them were sexually involved with the women and that they believed it was "morally right." When the superintendent attempted to get the cottage to create a rule prohibiting sexual intercourse, the men refused, saying they would not as a community enforce it, although they understood that the prison discipline board would have to deal with incidents "it became aware of." Luckily, this gulf between inmates and staff was the program's exception rather than its norm. Inmates generally maintained the social contract of the cottage, provided they felt a sense of genuine mutuality with the rest of the community and believed the decisions they arrived at were not coerced or manipulated by the staff.

Both the sense of openness of the democratic group and the willingness of inmates to enforce cottage rules were highly related to the manner in which the staff *presented* issues to the group for resolution. Even practical maintenance issues, officers learned, had to be transformed into issues of fairness within the group. A staff member imploring *"Please* clean the hopper closet" was apt to be much less effective than one raising the moral issue of "Everybody has been scrubbing her fingers to the bone except Betty Sue, who sat on her duff all week."

To be effective, staff members also had to learn to be genuinely sensitive to the differences in life perspective between them and the inmates. Officers repulsed by homosexuality, for example, had little chance of effectively mediating a homosexual conflict. Staff members who showed repugnance toward drug use could not encourage inmates to even attempt to enforce the cottage drug rules.

Airing and Resolving Conflicts

The second major function of community meetings was the airing and resolution of conflicts among members of the cottage. These sessions were designed to be more than just gripe or catharsis sessions, for the Just Community program required that both the process of resolving conflicts and the resolutions themselves appear fair and equitable to all community members. An example of the conflict resolution process may be seen in a dispute in which a somewhat inexperienced male staff member, Jones, defended a white female inmate attacked by a young black woman and was accused in community meeting by another woman, Eve, of "only sticking up for whitey." Two other black women, Joan and Ann, sought to make Jones understand Eve's position and to make Eve consider Jones' actions in the light of his past impartiality toward both black and white women.

Eve:	I just want to say, Jones, that I think you're prejudiced.
Jones (staff):	Well, you've got to give me something to go on.
Eve:	OK, I'm gonna give you something to go on, but 'cause I know you know what I'm talking about, I don't have to give you so much to go on. . . . I told you

about it before with Barb in that incident with Barb. It seems that you just take up for white people, and, to me, you're just like that. It just seems like you're prejudiced.

Jones: Can I . . .

Eve: I'm awfully sorry, Jones, that's the impression you give me. That's the way I feel, and nuthin's gonna change my feelings. Everything that comes off with you, the expression on your face, as I sit right here and look right at you . . . your whole appearance and everything about you is prejudiced to me. And that's just the way I feel; those are my feelings.

Joan: The way I see Jones, I see Jones as for the underdog. No matter who they are, Jones gonna promise to save the day, you know. I really do, and that's 'cause we ain't never really hot on you, Eve, and you know that, like we should be. Anybody can hot on you, anybody can hot on me, OK? But this just don't happen, the two who get hollered on, the most happen to be white, the way I see it, because Jones, he came to the defense of Minnie [black inmate] when we were getting on her so much. I just see him going for the underdog all the time. He is going to make sure the underdog gets their say.

Eve: . . . I looked at what he just said. Maybe he is sticking up for the underdog; I still got the impression that he's prejudiced, maybe in his own little way 'cause I'm prejudiced, in my own little way . . . it might be me . . . OK? But then, I don't hate all white people. There is some I get along with, there is some I just don't.

Joan: It's not the white race that you're prejudiced [toward]. You're prejudiced toward certain people.

Eve: Ah, no, I'm not prejudiced to all, but just to some, I am, you know, Jones. I like Jones, so I don't think it's because I'm prejudiced that I fired on him. I think he got a little prejudice in him, too.

Ann: Everybody do. Everybody. It's just that Jones should be shown.

The two black women's efforts to convince Eve that Jones really is not "any more prejudiced" than she is seem to be at least partly successful. Although she still feels Jones has a little prejudice in him, Eve seems satisfied that the group has dealt with her concern. Ann, too, feels the issue has been explored sufficiently to offer, in summary, that Jones is basically all right, but he must "be shown" by the community how to act in the meetings.

Similar dynamics were observed in community meetings arbitrating disputes between inmates as well as between inmates and staff. As the literature of the inmate subculture in traditional prisons attests—Sykes (1958) or Clemmer (1940)—inmate relationships only rarely surface to the view of staff. Inmates seldom share with their custodians the secret dynamics of inmate power, respect, and loyalty. While the secrecy and covertness of the traditional prison culture often dominated the Just Community units' social life, at times the inner dynamics of the cottage subculture emerged openly in community meetings when inmates decided to use the meetings to arbitrate disputes. This occurred when there seemed to be a reasonable degree of trust within the community and inmates felt the staff could be trusted to help them with their interpersonal relationships.

An example of this involved a male inmate named Mick who had been living with his "old lady," Sally, while outside but on arriving at the prison began a jailhouse romance with a long-term female offender named Molly. Three months later, Sally was arrested, was sent to Niantic, and discovered the affair. The men's cottage community became aware of the problem because Mick had not been doing anything, not even bothering to attend small groups. Bill is a staff member.

Corte (staff):   Smith tells me you been really fucked up, Mick, that you're not doing your house assignment. You want to tell the group about it?

Mick: It's something I decided to tell the group about, not just small group, but here. You know how broads are in here. I just laid around and laid around listening to music. I just said, fuck it, man, pass the time away. I forgot about making something of this shit. . . . I talked to Bill. He told me that one of them would get

	hurt. . . . I told my street lady [Sally] that I laid this other broad. . . . I dig her, really. . . . It's nothing, though, that I could settle down with. . . .
Smith:	Either you make a choice, or it get made for you. (Long pause)
Ed:	What if Molly says, "Bye-bye?" Could you deal with that?
Mick:	Yah. I gotta tell her it's over.
Todd:	How would you feel if she said, "It's over"?
Mick:	Bad.
Zeke:	What do you think you owe Molly if you tell her?
Mick:	Nothing.
Al:	An explanation?
Mick:	Nothing.
Sands (staff):	I disagree. You entered into it blind. You messed up, you gotta clean up.
Ed:	She knew what she was getting into. What does he owe her?
Fats:	Are you waiting for one of them to get sprung? That would solve the whole problem. You could have the other one.
Sands:	I don't know, Mick, but when you enter into a relationship and you end it, you owe an explanation. Like, if I tell Smith we're gonna have a beer and something comes up, then I gotta tell him something. No?
Smith:	Instead of dealing with two broads, he lays up. That don't do nothing for him or the house. It's ruining him. Right back when he was on the streets.
Al:	Look, this is just a jailhouse trip. On the streets, he could have both broads . . .
Sands:	What you gonna do, Mick?
Mick:	Tell her [Molly] and tell her why.

Mick, in fact, did formally terminate his relationship with Molly and offered her his affection for Sally as his reason. Whether the termination was merely a formality remained highly questionable.

Cliques frequently came under the scrutiny of the community meetings. One such group in the women's model cottage began hoarding food for its members, which came to light when a staff member found a bag of sweet rolls in an inmate's room. In the community meeting, this discovery revealed the following:

Smith (staff): We did a room search and found a huge bag of sweet rolls in Evie's room. Can you tell us why it was there?

Evie: I was saving it for Ann, Barb, Edie, and Sal. Sal, you know, is pregnant.

(House breaks into hysterical laughter.)

Jones (staff): I see a great deal of mistrust in here. This house lacks trust all over. . . . You don't trust each other enough to believe if you don't go grabbing, that you won't get two eggs in the morning.

Edie: I don't like it. . . . But that's the way it is. . . .

Alta: What if I stole all the cereal?

Edie: I would have stopped you!

Alta: Why didn't anybody stop Evie?

Irene: I see a big division. . . . It's the Oldies versus the Newies.

Birdie: I agree. I think Evie and Niki, for example, have feelings that aren't coming out. . . .

Alicia: I feel things are being held back, too. . . .

Smith: Is it between Evie and Niki, or Oldies versus Newies . . . ?

Evie: It ain't a big division. . . . I talk to new women.

Niki: I don't see it, Evie. Do you really try to meet new women?

Smith: What do new women feel?

Toni: They smile at you, then talk behind your back.

Monica: I feel uneasy in here.

Jones: What are we going to do about this?

Evie: I guess we gotta work in small group. . . .

Niki: That won't change shit, but you gotta try. . . .

The resolution of social conflict in community meetings made uncommon demands on staff members, requiring at times the skill of counselors and sociologists as well as ethical philosophers. Moreover, they were required to convey a great deal of trust, both in themselves and in the group as a whole. In addition, they were required to have a clear picture of the inmate group as a social system: who was going with whom, who the "honchos" were, who was angry at whom, and so on. Finally, they had to be able to offer ways of resolving conflicts that were substantively just and were perceived as such by both staff and inmates.

The success of community meetings in resolving inmate conflicts varied. At times, the inmate underlife would remain hidden, and the meetings would be unenthusiastic and would end quickly. At other times, the inmates would allow their relationships and hopes to be dealt with openly and freely, and then the Just Community ideal achieved a moment of reality.

Marathon Meetings

Thomas Jefferson declared that no constitutional society should go twenty years without a revolution. The Just Community programs, however, mandated a "revolution" every twelve weeks, at a "marathon meeting," which usually lasted the better part of a day (sixteen hours was the longest), in which the old constitution was abolished and new rules created. Marathon sessions served a number of purposes, one of them being to force each successive group of inmates to go through the process of the first days of the program. Over the years, the reality of the first constitution receded from the inmates' consciousness, and by 1972 there was no inmate still in prison who had participated in the first negotiations. Because the reasons for the program were obscure to the later inmates, occasionally one of the older inmates would be asked during the marathon to tell the group how the program was started. In some marathons, there were only minor additions and deletions made in the cottage rules; these mostly served to orient inmates to the ritual of creating constitutional rules. Other marathons involved great conflict or a reorientation of the program. In one meeting, for instance, there was a stormy debate about whether or not to require expulsion of an inmate after twice being caught with contraband. This was during a period of widespread drug use in the prison in general, including the model units, as well as growing mistrust between staff and inmates and breakdown in community morale. To everyone's surprise, Toni, a long-term drug-user, urged the more draconian rule:

Bea: I feel you got to give a woman a chance.

Toni: I feel if you give a drug fiend that space she will use it.

Barb: If I had a chance to use drugs and not get bounced, I would do it.

Ruth: If you have an overly harsh penalty, not all the stuff will come to group. No one will bring a drug thing downstairs knowing someone could get sent out of here.

Toni: You all have never shot dope the way I did. No *real* dope fiend is gonna bring it up, no matter what.

Mimi: Are you saying that, Toni, because you are going home? What if you had to live here eight or nine more months?

Toni: No, that's not it. Look at Jackie and what she said [Jackie had just been expelled for drug use]: "They allowed me to do it." That's it: By being easy, we allow people to mess up!

Doris: I agree with Toni. If a person comes here looking for help, you gotta be firm.

Dot: I feel they should be allowed one mistake. They should be given one chance, then out.

Toni: You already had your mistake. You are in jail!

Mimi: But if they get thrown out of here, they could get a new criminal charge behind it, just for a weed.

Bea: They don't think about no expulsion or no case. A dope fiend just acts. She doesn't think.

Gert: I don't see it. You can't put a dope fiend in jail and tell them no dope; it won't work.

Typically, the marathon meeting voted for "Frontstreet" to accept an increase in power of the cottage. After the group agreed that a new rule or privilege was reasonable, the unit supervisor and we ourselves (the authors) negotiated the matter with the Niantic superintendent. Often, proposals of this type were negotiated back and forth, with revisions demanded by both sides, before the change was accepted. In the following marathon, Green (unit supervisor) reported that he had sought to play an advocate role for the cottage with the prison administration over a request for late-night privileges once a week (watching television) until 1:30 A.M. on Saturday.

Green (staff):   They felt they couldn't give us a privilege they couldn't give the entire institution . . . and if it

	worked out here they didn't know how it would work out in Davis [maximum security]. . . . So, when they were ready to consider it for the entire institution, they would let us try.
Barb:	That is stupid! In the model cottage, we would be the first, and if it works out here . . . how come they don't give us a try?
Monica:	Should Green ask for them [privileges] or wait 'til we make some progress?
Barb:	I don't think we have grown far enough or gone far enough that we should get it. Now. . . .
Sue:	What have we done? We went so far downhill [a series of homosexually oriented cliques had dominated the cottage for a time], and we are just getting ourselves together. We have been doing this for one stinking week, and we are going to go to them and say we proved ourselves for a week. . . .
Barb:	I am bored! . . . my vocal cords are getting tired.

Several inmates urged a vote be taken; others urged the group wait on pushing the request for late-night privileges.

Monica:	I agree on waiting!
Barb:	That way we got something to work for.
Cheri:	Do we have to keep on waiting 'til the other girls prove themselves? Green proposed it, and they listened, and now we say we will wait. So we are uncertain? . . . Do we have to show everybody that?
Barb:	I feel we should wait, if it is ninety-nine years. . . . I was here in October [when the unit opened] and I have been bugging about TV privileges since I got here, but let's wait.
Bea:	Take a vote on waiting!
Green:	How about if we bring it up and she approves; and then we decide to hold it?
Barb:	As a matter of fact, Green, I think you should try to get it approved and just hold onto it. Don't you think that

would make people work twice as hard, knowing that
Green has it and is holding onto it?

Cheri: I disagree; I still think Green should get it approved now.

Bea: Like Green said, we will be the ones holding onto it, and I
feel if we are the ones holding onto it, then we will work
harder. Let's have a show of hands on who feels we should
wait.

   Some marathons revealed serious tensions between the cottage
staff and inmates, and on at least four occasions the cottage staff
retracted powers originally given to the inmates. Once, in the
women's program, staff members ruled autocratically for nearly a
month, explaining they were "fed up with the inmates' irresponsibil-
ity and [inability to] enforce their own rules." The contractual basis
for such revocations was tenuous, but, as the program supervisor
announced at one marathon, "Listen, ladies, I'm making this
decision not on a program basis, but on an institutional one. You are
not capable of living up to the democracy, so I'm going back to the
way it was before 1971."

   The inference that the democracy could be revoked unilaterally by staff was a perennial issue at the marathons. One time an
inmate noted (correctly) that the program was a "half-democracy." In
another session, the inmates threatened to "democratically vote the
staff to be dictators" unless they accepted new group power. These
discussions about the limits of cottage democracy, although frustrat-
ing, were critical to the program's survival, for without such dialogue
and qualification, inmates would soon have become disillusioned.
The marathons served to define the program's boundaries, even at the
expense of shattering illusions as to the limitlessness of the democracy, but in order to discover the possibilities for democratic action,
the inmates and staff had to have a clear statement of limits. Despite
the difficulties, however, marathons were conducted in a festive spirit
and with a general feeling of goodwill.

   One ritual developed during the marathons that later took
place when an inmate was ready to leave the program. First, community members would take turns expressing their feelings about the
inmate, and after this round robin the individual would express his or
her feelings about leaving the community. Here, for instance, are the

thoughts of one woman anticipating release to the program's halfway house, where she had been once before, prior to being sent back to Niantic for violating a house rule:

> I don't want to live in luxury . . . but I want to be able to walk down the street and go somewhere and do things that I never done before. When I went to that halfway house, the things I done that one week I was there, I have good feelings about it, because I did things in that halfway house that I haven't done for years. Guys coming up, "Let's play baseball," and so on, go to the dance, and go walk down the street, buying pizza—laughed all the way home, kicked our shoes off. And little things like that made me so happy, and I really hated to come back. And it was a lot of little things that I did that really made me feel good, like picking flowers in the park—real stupid things like that, but I really enjoyed it.
>
> But now that I have a little better feeling about myself, I know now what it means—that it's not just looking in the mirror, not fancy clothes and makeup and hairdos, that's not what I want to see. I just want to look at myself and say, "Wow, you are good people," not, "You are crazy and a clown," and . . . I thought about this in lockup. Life is worth living. Dark days have bright tomorrows. That is what I have found. Too many people just never look around; they go through life never looking . . . [at the real meaning of things]. And when they finally look, they ask if tonight [or] today is the day before tomorrow.

Small Groups

Whereas community meetings and marathons dealt explicitly with community issues, small groups dealt with individual and personal issues.

There were a variety of small groups. In some, using techniques of peer counseling we taught them, inmates counseled other inmates. In others, inmates and staff tried to resolve moral dilemmas occurring in the model cottage. In still others, inmates discussed current events or black literature or conducted formal debates. Whatever the orientation, each small group sought to create a "micro" moral community in prison.

The most common small group was that in which inmates helped each other resolve personal conflicts in their lives. Although every aspect of residents' lives was discussed, the most common topics were perhaps life, parenting, relationships with families, peer counseling, and the straight versus the criminal life. An illustration of how this group worked is seen in the case of one group in which Nan, a white inmate, arrived upset because she learned she was carrying the baby of a black man and her parents had demanded she give the baby up for adoption. As the following excerpt shows, the group sought to help to clarify the realistic options available to her:

Joan: Nan, what's the matter? Your folks come?

              (No response from Nan, who is quietly sobbing)

Sue Ann: What happened on your visit, huh?

Joan: They don't want the baby? They want you to have an abortion or what? Give him away?

Nan: Give him up.

Sue Ann: So what do you think about that?

Nan: I don't know because . . . he [Nan's father] had a lot of things to say about . . .

Sue Ann: I can imagine what he had to say.

Nan: I guess I always respected him . . .

Sue Ann: All that is due to the fact that the baby is supposed to be mixed, right?

Nan: Mostly.

Sue Ann: Did you know that your parents were prejudiced before you started messing around with a black guy?

Nan: Yeah.

Sue Ann: That didn't make any difference?

Nan: To me?

Sue Ann: Yeah, and you never thought that at any time, when you were going with him, what the outcome might be if you did get pregnant, what your situation would be? You never even thought about that, huh?

Joan: Well, Nan, the only thing I can say is that if you plan on going on your own, and having responsibility to yourself and not depending on your family for anything, I would say have the baby and truck it along. But if you are going to have to get some kind of help or [you're] going to your family, I think the best thing you could do, under those circumstances, is do as they say. But if you are responsible enough to go out there and make it on your own, keep the child.

Nan: I know that, but see, he said that he doesn't . . . he thinks having the baby and keeping it is going to, um . . . that I won't be able to do it, and, um, and . . . as far as school and getting through high school and, like, getting a job, he said it is all going to go down the drain if I keep the baby.

Joan: Anyway, he's about right, because when you have a baby the party time is over. There is no more party times. The party is over if you're going to be a proper mother. But like I say, anybody can have a child, but everybody can't be a mother.

Sue Ann: What I am saying is I don't think that that's what her father means as far as it is "all going to go down the drain." The only thing that I can see her father objecting about is that her baby is going to be mixed. That's what they are saying to her, that she is not going to be able to make it because of that. That is going to be a hindrance to her whether she has her education or not. They don't want no part of it, so they can't see why anybody else would want any part of it.

Joan: This is what I am saying, if she's got it in her mind she wants this child—in other words, "Hell what my family says; I want this baby and I am going to take care of this baby"—she can go ahead and do it and don't need her family to do nothing for her.

The key to the success of the group here was the inmates' acceptance of the authenticity of Nan's dilemma and their ability to maintain authentic respect and concern for her. Inmates in small groups were understandably more responsive, empathetic, and non-judgmental than were some staff members in similar situations. For example, although a female staff member named Smith, while listening to an inmate named Irma describe how she felt about prostitution, was quite skillful, another staff member, Davis, clearly misinterpreted Irma's remarks as meaning she needed help—thereby undercutting the group's effectiveness as it turned its attention from Irma to Davis.

Irma:	Everybody knows that hustling is the best money in the world.
Smith (staff):	Do you want to do that the rest of your life?
Irma:	No, I'm not going to say that I want to do it the rest of my life, but I will say I like that business. And I will say I'm going back to school and I'm going to get as much out of it as I can, and I'm going to get me a good job, but I'm still going to keep my little buddies on the side, because that will be my pocket money. Because I like nice things, I like to live good, and I like to have money.
Smith:	But is that living good?
Irma:	Yes, it's living good because it's good money, and I'm serious. You just try to talk somebody out of a hundred dollars, you've got to know what you're doing. But, I mean, I can't see standing downtown turning tricks for ten and fifteen dollars, you know. The tricks, they put you through so much bullshit. I mean [if] you have to do everything for ten or fifteen dollars for all kinds of ugly men and everything, I couldn't do it.
Davis (staff):	I'd like to ask a question, Mrs. Smith. I'm quite serious about helping Irma with her problem. I think Irma has been quite open with her feelings; so we all have a right to our way of life. So, who's going to counsel? . . . how are we going to counsel Irma on how to change?
Irma:	But I don't want to change . . .
Marge:	Forget it, Irma . . .
	(Pause)
Sally:	Mrs. Smith, I'd like to request a furlough.

Helping inmates work through personal moral dilemmas required skill on the part of the group leader, who needed to be able to listen actively to the individual's concerns and to re-pose the problem as a moral issue. An example of this skill may be seen in the following group, led by Smith, in which Jerrie had asked if she should admit to a parole board that when she got out she intended to see Arlene, an ex-inmate from Niantic, despite the parole board's previously prohibiting this.

Jerrie:	When I go before that man, I'm not gonna lie to him about it.
Ann:	But what if he sets you back [rejects her request for parole]? Why not just try and fudge around the subject? . . . Then you will be out.
Lynn:	I agree, I wouldn't tell him nothing. There was this broad who used to be here. Mr. Raines [parole board chairman] asked her if she was going to blow some herb when she got out. She said she would. He set her back.
Smith (staff):	What do the rest of you feel? Would it be right to lie to get out of jail, like Ann is arguing?
Kay:	Look, it's your freedom. I wouldn't tell.
Jerrie:	But he's going to find out. Then you are out and get violated for something you could have straightened out from the beginning.
Nan:	I agree with Jerrie; it's not right to lie, even to Mr. Raines. It's not worth it. You'd feel bad, even as you walked free through those gates.
Kay:	I wouldn't feel so bad. I'd feel fine.

Eventually Jerrie decided to tell the parole board the truth about Arlene.

The most effective advice we could give staff and inmates in small groups was simply, "Ask questions." For instance, when Jan wanted to leave the program, a well-timed officer's question was able effectively to focus the discussion:

Jan:	I want to leave.
Louise:	Why?
Jan:	I ain't getting nothin' here. No one talks in group. I'm bored.

Louise: It's real quiet in here, sometimes.
Smith (staff):   Can I ask a question, Jan? What do you think you owe
                   the group in this decision?
Jan: Huh?
Doris: Like, have you done everything you can? Could you
                   help?
Jan: No, really.

Small group had two justifications, sociological and psychological. The sociological rationale was that it created a context of
trust, almost like a surrogate family, in which inmates felt able to
express their doubts and hopes freely and openly. In its ideal form,
inmates and staff created a contract of mutual interdependence, with
each person seeking to help others with the expectation of being
helped in return. Of course, the constraints against such an ideal
community were many: Staff and inmates came from radically different worlds, and the former often had as much trouble understanding
drugs and the street life as the latter did comprehending car payments
and Sunday teas.

The psychological rationale for small groups has three parts.
First, in training inmates to be each other's counselors and forcing
them to take others' parts, we were proceeding from the idea that role
taking of another has been clinically associated with the development
of moral thinking (Dowell, 1972). By empathizing with another
according to this suggestion, a person is almost forced to take a Stage
3 as opposed to a Stage 2 moral position; in a Stage 3 position, the
concerns and needs of others are actively considered along with one's
own needs. Put in other terms, the small group model assumed that
people learn as much from counseling as from being counseled.

Second, it was assumed small groups would facilitate inmate-
inmate and inmate-staff moral dialogue as in the Cheshire study
described in Chapter Three. In the group dealing with whether or not
Jerrie should lie to her parole board, for instance, a real-life problem
was transformed into a moral one. The inmates were forced to try to
resolve the question of when it was right to lie, not as an academic
exercise but as one directly related to Jerrie's life. Through natural
and repeated dialogue, it was hoped that the inmates would gradually
change both the logical structure of their present ideology as well as

to reflect on some of its assumptions. An inmate would thus discover that there were perspectives of care and trust of which he or she might not have been aware. In addition, it was hoped, the inmate would discover visions of life that were unexplored.

Finally, small groups sought to hold members to their stated ideology. For example, one inmate declared that she had learned to care about her kids but then proceeded while on furlough to "get high" and not even visit them. On her return, her small group sought to explore with her the glaring contradictions between her ideology and her actions. This pressure on the individual to change, be it noted, comes not at the instigation of a leader in the service of either society or the institution but rather from the moral consensus developed by the inmates themselves. Thus, it was only when the small group acted as a voluntary institution of mutual trust that it could affect either judgment or action.

The three institutions of the Just Community program required constant training and reinterpretation to remain effective and meaningful to staff and inmates. The dilemmas of keeping such demanding institutions functioning in the face of the serious constraints of the prison are explored in Chapter Seven. However, first let us explore the initial research results obtained from the program.

6

Results of the Prison Experiment

Funding had not allowed us to undertake a scientifically rigorous research effort, but we were able to initiate a small research project to try to answer the following four questions about inmates in the Just Community program:

1. *Did inmates accept the model cottage rules and discipline procedures as fair and legitimate?* Many penologists assume that inmates almost necessarily experience alienation toward any prison environment, that the very fact of incarceration creates an adversary relationship between prisoner and prison. Hypothesizing that this alienation was not necessarily inevitable, we suggested that the Just Community cottage could be structured so that most inmates, as they understood them at their stage of moral development, would accept the community's rules as being fair and legitimate.

2. *Did inmates of different moral stages have unique conceptions of the program's rules and goals?* Because developmental theory suggests that people of different moral stages perceive social rules and norms in qualitatively discrete ways, we speculated that inmates of different moral stages understood the Just Community program in

quite different ways. We wondered if the community meetings, rules, and small groups were comprehensible to inmates and, if they were perceived differently by different inmates, how they were understood.

3. *Would a democratic prison environment change inmate moral thinking?* It had long been assumed (Kohlberg, 1971) that the social environment was related to moral change, but this had never been demonstrated in a natural setting. We wanted to see whether inmates who perceived the program as fair changed in their moral judgment and whether those who perceived it less positively did not change. This problem can be understood both as an examination of the relationship between the prison social environment and moral reasoning as well as an exploration of the possible use of the prison moral atmosphere in the moral reeducation of the offender.

4. *Did inmates emerge with different life goals from those they had when they entered prison?* We wondered whether the inmate's experience in the Just Community program would translate into commitment in the larger society. Although a careful recidivism study was not possible, we hoped to describe some of the relevant patterns in the transition from prison to outside.

We consider the initial answers to these four questions in the rest of this chapter.

How Inmates Perceived the Program's Rules

To tentatively answer our first question, twelve inmates each were randomly selected from the men's and women's model cottage projects. The women were matched with twelve subjects from a traditional cottage in Niantic according to age, race, crime, and length of sentence. The men were similarly matched with inmates from three contrasting male prisons. These control groups were established in order to compare inmate perceptions of the men's Just Community program with inmate perceptions of other prison programs emphasizing punitive custody, psychotherapy, and behavior modification treatments.

An experimental method of scoring environment perceptions, called the Moral Atmosphere Scoring System (MASS), was developed by one of us (Scharf). The instrument involved a lengthy interview probing inmate perceptions of programs, goals, rules, inmate roles, and staff norms. Criteria were developed for each aspect of moral atmosphere to determine if the inmate accepted, rejected, or was ambivalent toward a particular aspect of moral atmosphere.

Trained interviewers were used in gathering the data for the study. Interviews were tape-recorded and transcribed, and the transcribed data analyzed by scorers from the Harvard University Laboratory of Human Development. Interviews were scored blind; scorers had no identification with the experimental project. An interjudge reliability of .81 was achieved among moral atmosphere raters.

Results of the Model Cottages. In scoring the perceptions of female inmates in the Just Community cottage, it was found that 75 percent accepted the fairness of the political structure of the cottage. Generally, inmates saw themselves as "authors" of the rules and thought them fairly enforced by inmates. As one inmate stated, "In here, you make the rules. It's not like someone is putting them down on you from above. The girls make them and make sure that they are fair to both sides, staff and women."

The cottage was seen by many of the inmates as a context for mutual aid and problem solving. As one inmate stated, when she had a problem, she would sit and think it over for a few days, then go talk to the other girls about it. Having to aid other inmates was also seen by inmates as an affirmative obligation to maintaining cottage rules. A woman described an inmate who would not go to work even though she was jeopardizing the work release she wanted: "I felt that if I loved Betty as much as I say I do, I wouldn't let her slide like that, because that wouldn't be really caring. So I called a [community group meeting] and told the staff member what she did. It was for her and the cottage." Even disciplinary decisions were perceived as being fair when they were democratically decided by the group: "When the group comes down on you it's different from when the guards do it." Overall, the female inmates' perceptions of the program were highly positive, and many of them expressed a deep concern for the cottage and the staff-inmate community.

Although the male inmates perceived the Just Community program as being far more prisonlike than female inmates did, most saw the discipline procedures as being generally fair. "At least in here you can tell your side of it," one inmate remarked. "It's not just 'lock 'em up,' like at Cheshire." In a typical comment, one inmate stated that staff members "were as fair as they could be expected, but they had to answer to Frontstreet [the administration]." The inmates felt an obligation to enforce the cottage rules, but saw this as necessary to maintain the "easy time" at Niantic rather than, as in the women's cottage, as a product of group commitment and concern. As one told the authors, "It's like this: Either you lock a dude, or the Man locks him. Lots of times, I say, 'Hey, I don't really agree with this, but it's either keep the rules tight or we're all back at Cheshire.'" Inmates tended to make more favorable comments about the perceived fairness of the democratic cottage's rules than they did about the level of trust or concern for either staff members or other inmates. For example, one inmate said, "It may be democratic, but you still don't turn your back on no one."

Comparisons with Other Prison Programs. When the model cottage inmate's perceptions were compared with those of inmates in other programs, the results were strikingly different. Model cottage female inmates perceived a group authorship of their cottage rules, whereas women in the custody cottage, not surprisingly, perceived the rules and discipline as sanctions imposed by the staff, rather than needed actions by inmates, and staff members were perceived as being benign but controlling ("They tell you nice first, but they tell you"). One inmate offered, "In here, they take care of you pretty good, but if the guard sees you doing something she tells you about it and makes you do what she wants. They don't beat you or nothing . . . but the rules is for the guards." There was also little evidence of group trust.

Men in the custody cottage perceived their environment as being overtly brutal and saw officer authority as being arbitrary and coercive. Many inmates were convinced that the prison justice system operated as a means to suppress inmate dissent, with rules being manipulable by the staff simply to "get" certain inmates. When asked if inmates had rights, one inmate offered, characteristically, "Yeah, we can take orders."

The behavior modification prison was generally regarded quite negatively, the point system being thought of as a scheme "to bribe you into being a good little patsy." Rules were often described as being "silly and Mickey Mouse" and the staff as "not really caring about us." Inmates rarely perceived reasons for the staff's taking away points or giving points, and the point system was seen as a game inmates had to play in order to get parole more quickly.

The rules of the Transactional Analysis prison were generally accepted by most of the inmates, although inmates tended to put their trust in a particular prison counselor rather than in the institution. Some inmates, however, believed rules were enforced differentially, depending on "what the counselor thought was your problem . . . like if you are acting on your Child or your Parent." Yet other inmates were quite positive and perceived the rules as lenient and benign. One inmate indicated, "When I first got here, I was getting ripped off because I didn't have a lock on my locker, and I think that is a fair rule because they are protecting someone else's property. . . . Just rules that are protecting other people."

The results tended to support our contention that inmates respond to fairness of treatment, even if they reject the fairness of the larger correctional and judicial process.

How Inmates of Different Moral Stages Perceived the Program

The prison's social reality of the inmates differs, obviously, from that of the staff members. We wondered if we could relate these differences in perception to differences in moral stage of the individuals involved. Theorists studying the development of political ideology have found dramatic differences in how people conceive of the rules and laws of political institutions and have explained them in terms of differences in social class, childhood socialization, age, sex, and IQ. In the case of prison inmates in the model cottage, we wondered if these differences might be explained in terms of differences in moral reasoning. To explore this, we held detailed moral atmosphere interviews with thirty inmates and qualitatively analyzed them.

We found that the perceptions of Stage 2 inmates were very different from those of higher-stage inmates. Whereas higher-stage inmates perceived the program goals in terms of changes in attitudes or ideas, lower-stage inmates almost universally understood the program in terms of behavioral control. One Stage 2 inmate, for example, saw the purpose of the cottage as "keeping you out of trouble"; one small group meeting was called, she felt, to teach inmates that "You can get killed for cussing." Higher-stage inmates, however, said the counseling groups were to teach people "to care or respect one another."

Stage 3 inmates perceived the purpose of the program as encouraging caring relationships among the residents and the staff. For instance, one Stage 3 inmate justified the discipline given a particularly troubling inmate as showing her that "she can't be concerned about only herself and still be respected by all of us." Relationships with other inmates and staff were similarly evaluated by such words as *caring, helpfulness, sincerity,* and *concern.* For example, one woman said she believed another inmate, accused of stealing, did not need punishment "because she was concerned and showed trust by letting it be brought out in group." Cottage counselors also were praised for "trying" and "caring" and for "listening" to inmates. Among Stage 3 inmates, it was not so much important that staff members actually help inmates as that they "showed concern."

Stage 4 inmates were far more critical than Stage 3 inmates of the model cottage and had much greater awareness of the difference between ideal goals and actual accomplishments of the program. As one inmate put it, "The idea of the cottage is good, but the inmates don't always live up to what they say." Commenting on the difficulty of achieving the program's goals, another inmate said, "The program is fantastic, but it's very hard to change, to get the women to live up to their responsibilities to the program." Still, these inmates understood that the program goals were to teach inmates "to accept responsibility."

Stage 4 inmates were also highly conscious of the ideological and political world apart from the cottage and were able to evaluate the prison in terms of the larger realities. One inmate, for example, stated that "The politicians [administrators] in Hartford are using the cottage to prove how liberal they are." Another analyzed some cottage rules as being "more communist than capitalist, in that all people get the same, no matter if you are a brain surgeon or a bum." These inmates were more interested than lower-stage inmates in the process of rule creation and change, and most saw themselves as being active creators of the rules—for example, "Joan, Ann, and I sat for two days going over the rules of the cottage and how we wanted to be treated."

In summary, the Stage 2 inmates evaluated social action in terms of punishment and reward criteria. They often seemed unaware of the Stage 3 norms that more mature inmates seemed to accept. They often seemed to miss the intentions of others and the social ideas grasped by higher-stage inmates.

Stage 3 inmates tended to evaluate actions in interpersonal terms—to gauge actions according to the attitudes of individuals rather than according to more objective consequences. They showed a marked lack of critical awareness as to the content of particular programs.

Stage 4 inmates tended to be more rationally critical than Stage 2 or 3 inmates and to evaluate the prison programs in terms of broader social principles and categories.

The staff followed a similar pattern. Stage 2 staff were unable to deal with an intentional community structure and withdrew from the program almost immediately. Stage 3 staff members, however, typically thought that the small groups, as opposed to community meetings, should be emphasized more in the program. They often believed that the program did too much "grouping" and not enough "one-to-one stuff." Stage 4 staff members tended to identify with the program and to insist the rules be fair but securely enforced. Their criticisms of the program were usually that the rules were not being taken seriously or that the inmates were "getting away with murder."

Differences in moral understanding were observable in nearly every aspect of the program and were particularly evident in a communications gap between most inmates and most staff members. When officers posed a Stage 4 argument against the use of contraband—"You shouldn't be smoking marijuana here; it's against the cottage rules!"—a Stage 2 inmate, who focused mostly on consequences to him- or herself, might respond, "The hell with the rules. I like to smoke dope, and there's less chance of me getting caught here than anywhere else."

This pattern was visible in many community meetings. The following discussion, involving a furlough for an inmate named Will, shows an almost classic Stage 2-Stage 4 confrontation:

Will (Stage 2):   I want a furlough.
Ed (Staff, Stage 4):   Why?

Will:	I want to get out.
Bob (Stage 3):	What have you learned here? Have you done anything about your attitude?
Jones (staff, Stage 4):	I don't think we should give Will his furlough. . . . He hasn't done anything we've asked him to. He's been busted twice with pot. . . . Then there was that stuff with Betty.
Will:	You never did like me, Jones. Why are you busting me today?
Phil (Stage 3):	Will, don't you care about what other people think of you?
Will:	No.

Inmates and staff members would often define justice in radically different ways. For instance, the following discussion about a female inmate's failure to report another's intention to escape shows the gap in perceptions as to what was fair:

Sue (Stage 3):	Why didn't you report Tina?
Louise (Stage 2):	It wasn't my business!
Daves (staff, Stage 3):	Weren't you concerned about Marci [who was raped by some friends of Tina's]?
Louise:	Marci can take care of Marci . . .
Daves:	I think this is pretty disgusting. At one time, women in here cared about one another. Not now. It's everyone for themselves . . .
Louise:	You think I did something wrong, Mrs. Daves?

In the Just Community program, there were not only typically no Stage 5 inmates, but there were also usually few Stage 4 inmates. Most of the officers were also Stage 4 rather than Stage 5. During one (rather positive) period in 1973, we systematically scored every person in the female cottage seeking to ascertain the moral ecology of the group, as shown in Table 6. As Table 6 shows, the community included a range of moral ideologies and a large gap between the average staff member and the average inmate. To remedy this dilemma, four strategies were developed:

Table 6. Predominant Moral Stage of Just Community
Participants, June 1973.

Stage	Supervisor	Officers	Inmates
1	—	—	1
2	—	—	8
3	—	2	10
4	1	3	2
5	—	1	—

1. The model cottage staff used (Stage 3 or 4) inmates to re-
interpret and communicate higher-stage communications for lower-
stage inmates. This worked very well—provided the higher-stage
inmates agreed with higher-stage staff members.

2. Staff members tried to use the moral education techniques
described in Chapter Three to communicate their ideas—that is, they
would interpret a Stage 4 position in Stage 2 or 3 terms. For example,
they might say, "Listen, fellas, we have rules here we believe should
be respected. If the community goes, then no more program. That
means fewer furloughs and goodies." However, this approach usually ended with inmates referring to the staff as "phony" and "manipulative" (among the kinder expletives).

3. Staff attempted to present higher-stage reasoning as carefully and clearly as possible in order that inmates might recognize
that Stage 4 ideas were fairer than were the Stage 2 ideas expressed by
their peers. This process took a great deal of time and patience.

4. The group was structured to include at least some Stage 4
and many Stage 3 inmates. This was always difficult, at times impossible, and it left us open to the charge of stacking the deck in the
program's favor. It also meant its results could not be generalized to
other prison situations (because it is unlikely that prisons have
mostly Stage 3 and 4 inmates).

All four strategies were used with varying degrees of success.
However—and this is an extremely important point—the program
showed great signs of distress whenever the majority of the inmates
did not possess at least *some* Stage 3 reasoning. It worked best when it
consisted of at least 50 percent conventionally Stage 3 and 4 inmates
who were respected by inmates and who identified with the most

reasonable positions of the officers. However, middle-class Stage 4 inmates were almost useless in helping to establish a genuine participatory community, being rejected by other inmates as "junior staff." The most positive leaders in maintaining the Just Community program were those inmates who were genuinely respected by other inmates and were higher-stage moral leaders as well.

How the Democratic Prison Changed Moral Judgment

To see if an environment perceived as just would stimulate moral thinking among inmates, we observed female participants in the first year of the Just Community experiment. Twenty-four model cottage inmates were selected at random and were matched, according to age, race, crime, and length of sentence, with ten women from a traditional cottage, eighteen men from an untreated control group, and eighteen men from a group engaging in intensive moral discussion in a traditional prison.

Effects of environments on moral reasoning were measured by using Kohlberg's Moral Maturity interview, which rates the logical structure underlying moral judgments, using a guide that defines stage-typical responses to various dilemmas as described in Chapter Three.

As in the moral atmosphere study described earlier, taped interviews were performed by two graduate students trained by Kohlberg and his colleagues at the Harvard University Laboratory of Human Development. The interviews were later transcribed and blind scored by Kohlberg personnel. Differences of .39 of one moral stage were found between pre- and posttest interviews (five months apart) among inmates under twenty-four years of age. This group was considered to be the "target" group, as longitudinal studies (Kohlberg, 1969) have indicated that moral reasoning tends to stabilize after age twenty-five. The degree of change was seen, therefore, as a sizable one, for nearly one-third of the group shifted more than half a moral stage—for example, from Stage 2 to Stage 2-3. This compared favorably with similar moral education efforts conducted with noncriminal populations (Kohlberg, Wasserman, and Richardson, 1975). The changes were statistically significant when compared with matched control groups in both male and female prisons and with members of the intensive moral discussion group in the traditional male prison (see Table 7).

Table 7. Changes (in MMS points) in Moral Reasoning Levels (One Stage = 100 MMS points).

Setting	Pretest	Posttest	Change
17 model cottage inmates (under 24 years old)[a]	260	299	+39
10 female prisoners, traditional cottage (control group)	270	268	− 2
18 male prisoners, traditional prison (control group)	254	256	+ 2
18 male prisoners from moral discussion groups in traditional prison (control group)	251	268	+17

Note: Analysis of variance procedures indicated significant differences at the .01 level.

[a]Of the remaining 7 inmates, 3 showed slight positive change, while 2 showed no change and 2 apparently regressed.

Inmates who changed in level of moral judgment generally had quite positive perceptions about the Just Community program. This was interesting because developmental research had long suggested that a change in moral thinking was associated empirically with identification with a positive social group. This relationship is evident when the perceptions of inmates who did not change in moral thinking are compared with those who changed markedly. For example, June and Sue, two women who morally regressed during their stay, perceived the model cottage program extremely negatively. June (who went from 282 pretest down to 255 posttest) stated, "I feel that these [moral development] theories are good in some cases, but not in all. Theories are for people in different societies, different parts of the world."

Sue (who went from 287 to 217) was even more cynical. For her, life was war, and so she felt it necessary to put on a front. Thus for Sue the program was essentially a big put-on. Asked what she got out of the model cottage, she said,

> I learned how to figure people a little better. . . . At different points, this house has gotten next to me in different ways . . . but so far as the bullshit is concerned, they couldn't

get nothing with that crap they were pulling. . . . Hell, I am going to front, I am going to go through my life fronting. . . . Until I find I can be open and honest with people, without taking the risk of getting hurt, until then, I am going to keep up my front. That's the way I know how to live. If I find a better way, then I will find that. . . . There is too many bull- shit people in here [the model cottage]. A lot of us talk about Pete and Joe [the authors] and shit as soon as they come out of those doors [leave]. . . . Like I could never trust the group with nothing, I don't care how long I stay here. I would have never told too much and anything I would have told . . . would be because they wanted to hear it.

In striking contrast were Ann and Kay's interviews. Ann saw herself personally transformed by the program: "I know it was the cottage, but a lot came from me. If I had been in another cottage, I would not be responsible as I have been. Here I knew if I did some- thing, I was not just hurting myself, it would affect everybody . . . like just staying out of work . . . and then I thought of what it would do to the cottage if everyone started taking days off, staying home. . . . People would say 'Ann is staying home, so why can't I?' . . . It's not because I would get punished, it's because I care more."

Kay was even more enthusiastic: "I found something in this cottage I was looking for a long time and that was understanding. Like I did a few things I got caught for, but there wasn't anybody condemning me like the police. . . . When I got caught, we talked it over, and I found a lot of understanding. . . . I found love in this house, not with everybody, but with a certain few."

Most of the morally changed inmates saw themselves as "authors" of the cottage rules. Kathy, for example, stated, "Stephanie and I sat for two days going over the rules of the cottage and how we felt we wanted to be treated, and that we didn't want to be treated as a prisoner, we wanted to be treated like human beings. . . . I feel this is the goal, and it has helped me quite a bit."

These results give some evidence that a prison may be used as a potential means for altering inmates' value systems, evidence lacking in earlier experiments with milieu therapy because there was no research tool for documenting changes in moral thinking as opposed to moral content. This distinction is critical, for it is easy for inmates to fake changes in the content of their values (for example, to say they don't believe in ripping off any more), but changes in the process of thinking are much more difficult to counterfeit. We had criticized the early innovators in the prison democratic reform movement for lacking an instrument to document whether democratic experience actually resulted in a change in democratic responsibility or understanding. The Kohlberg measure suggests a new psychological technology for measuring the capacity for democratic thinking. This initial study tends, first, to support Kohlberg's assertion that moral change is associated with the perception of justice in the environment and, second, to strengthen the contention that the social environment of the prison might be used as a means of political reeducation.

The Effect of the Program on Inmate Lives After Prison

Preliminary results of a two-year study indicate the model cottage program in general has had an apparent positive effect on female inmates' lives after they left prison. Although these results are only first indications of a necessarily small sample of twenty inmates and do not directly link moral stage change with successful life adjustments, they are nevertheless hopeful signs of overall program efficacy. Official recidivism figures for the Niantic population do not exist. Therefore, we conducted a cross-sectional study of 100 former prisoners, one year after release, which indicated a 35 percent recidivism rate, including parole violations. For the 20 female model cottage graduates, however, less than 15 percent returned to Niantic after one year with either a new charge or for parole violations. In general, recidivism for prisoners as a whole follows a decreasing geometric pattern over time; most of those returned to prison committed a serious crime within six months after their release, and the proportion drops thereafter. This implies that our figures after an average of two years are probably relatively stable, although it remains for a controlled study, to be done over five years, to confirm these findings.

Of the inmates returning to prison quickly, many were among those in the lowest moral stages. Hanna, a seventeen-year-old (Stage 1), the lowest-stage inmate in the program, returned to her middle-class black family in Hartford, remained less than one week, and then spent the next few weeks on the streets. Found beaten and hungry by her parole officer, she refused to move into a halfway house, yet agreed to live with Debby, an older ex-inmate and program graduate, but after five weeks she ran away and after a week or so of "hustling" was arrested for slugging a Pinkerton officer who had caught her shoplifting.

Other inmates' parole violations seemed related to long-term self-destructive personal dynamics not affected in any way by the program. Peggy (Stage 3) moved in with an old boyfriend who was a dope dealer, was twice arrested when police raided his apartment, and finally admitted she was shooting heroin and was pregnant. More or less by mutual consent, she agreed to be returned for parole violation for three months in order to get out of a situation she apparently could not handle and also to persuade the prosecutor not to press charges on her two arrests.

Midge, a drug addict for over ten years, was "stipulated" to a drug program against her wishes as a condition of her release. She informed the board of her reservations about the drug program, based on her prior experience with it, and stated that the model cottage had helped her with her problem. The board was adamant, because of her long-repeated drug violations. Shortly after her arrival, she left the program, remained drug-free for several weeks, notified the police of her whereabouts, and simply waited for a reluctant parole officer to pick her up.

The majority of women who managed to stay out of prison more than a year often were able to find some noncriminal tie. For Sue, who moved from Stage 2 to 3-2, it was the availability of a recreation center in her community: "You can dance, sing, laugh," she reported. "It's better than the street. You don't need drugs." Others found that their parents were willing to accept them back into a supportive family network. "When I came out, all my family was real good to me," Emily said. "They took me back in, no matter what happened. Now all I care about is them, my family and brothers and sisters."

For a woman who had spent nearly ten years as a prostitute (Stage 3-2 to 4-3), it was getting married. "We lived together since we met and got married in April. We decided to make it legal. It's not perfect, and we got to pull each other up. . . . [Once he] went shopping and came back with two pepperoni [pizzas]. They were $4.19 each. He said he bought them. I remembered that he only had $4.

'How,' I asked, 'did you get $8 worth of groceries for $4?' I looked at
the slip and found more than $4 more groceries than we had. I told
him he was a damn liar. I put the pepperoni in the bag and went back
to the A&P and told the man. . . . We pull each other up . . . like
group."

Religion also seems to have been an important factor in the
women who stayed out of prison. "I found this Jesus thing," one
inmate who moved from Stage 2 to 3-2 said. "I write letters to the
Jesus people. Sometimes I talk to myself in the bathroom. I talk to
Him. I couldn't have made it without Him." Another simply said, "I
went back to the Bible thing my mother told me about when I was
little."

Finding a meaningful job or educational program was obviously an important factor in determining readjustment. The inmates
who found jobs that offered a sense of positive community and
purpose almost invariably avoided further imprisonment. The
majority of the successful first-year model cottage graduates found
stable jobs with some responsibility. For instance, three began running drug rehabilitation programs. One woman found a job as a
controller. Several others finished college.

The successful inmates' recollections of the model cottage
program were quite different from those of inmates who remained in
a street existence. The latter tended to perceive the program as not
being very effective, whereas the former remembered the cottage
fondly, and even eulogistically. One inmate said, "Well, I learned to
care about people. I also learned to care about me. I have always put
me second best. . . . When I got out, I found myself using what I
learned there, as far as ways of dealing with things." Another offered,
"The thing I liked there was that you could say what was on your
mind, no matter what it was. They didn't get mad at you. Sometimes
they would put you on the floor, but they would always pick [you]
up."

It is still premature to judge the efficacy of the Just Community program in terms of the adjustment of its graduates. Until a
carefully matched control group is followed for five years after
release, comparisons must serve only heuristic, rather than evaluative,
purposes. This work is presently underway. Even were a carefully
controlled experiment to be available, recidivism data would have to

be scrutinized carefully. Like any educational program, a prison program experience represents only one influence on a complex life process. Just as it would be unreasonable to expect six years at Summerhill or four years at college to retrieve an otherwise damaged life, it is similarly so to expect a prison program to permanently redirect its graduates' lives.

Family, peers, faith, meaning, work are all important influences. For the average doctor, lawyer, banker or college teacher to become a pimp, junkie, prostitute, shoplifter, or con artist would mean he or she would have to reject past social alliances and develop new skills and ties. Such change obviously requires the support of people willing to welcome the change into a new life-style; without such support, it is unrealistic to expect meaningful alterations in behavior. However, the Just Community program offered a beginning for inmates to assume new meaning in their lives as well as new ties and a sense of community. When future ties and community were available and accepted, the inmates' changes became permanent. When they were unavailable or rejected, the Just Community program was simply a transitory experience.

7

Constraints on Reform

Democratic prison programs have hardly been notable for their longevity. As Thomas Murton (1976) has observed, most such reforms die out or are terminated in four or five years. Maconochie's Norfolk Island experiment, for example, lasted only four years. Osborne lasted less than two years at Sing Sing. After eight years, we personally understood the many reasons for the short life expectancy of a prison democracy.

"Building a democracy in a prison," a friend of ours observed, "is as futile as building a sand castle at low tide. . . . You can hold the sea out sometimes, but it always gets through, one way or another." The tide in this case was the reestablishment of autocratic prison rules and the reemergence of mutual mistrust and exploitation.

As we mentioned earlier, the key constraints against any successful effort at the democratization of the prison include the following:

1. The cycles of trust implicit in any community enterprise with necessarily transient membership
2. The conflict between bureaucratic correctional organization and an inmate participatory democracy

3. The lack of legitimate economic or political power available to the inmates as opposed to that available to the administration and staff
4. The meaninglessness of consent in the context of the prison, where the choice of participating in a democratic prison program is often made without there being other viable choices
5. The lack of legal status given the inmate-staff democracy

Let us review these constraints to see how they affected our democratic prison community at Niantic.

Cycles of Community Trust

The Niantic model cottage program was never a completely stable social community. This was largely due to the highly transient nature of many prison populations, in general. The average term for women at Niantic, for example, is approximately nine months. Cheshire inmates remain incarcerated slightly longer. Additionally, inmates serving jail sentences within the general prison population at Cheshire and Niantic presented additional problems. Since the length of their sentences is statutorily fixed and limited to a year or less, they tend to view incarceration as a temporary inconvenience. Thus, joining special projects such as the Just Community is more often motivated by a desire to be with friends or enjoy perceived program benefits than to invest themselves in program objectives. Finally, there was the practical necessity during overcrowded times of temporarily housing nonprogram members in the model unit. As a result of one or more of these factors, a cottage unit could and did move from relative calm and a seemingly cohesive sense of community to the brink of chaos and back in just a few months. Consider one six-month period in the women's model cottage program. A log entry from the women's program in the spring of 1975 summarizes the general sense of well-being held by the staff, inmates, and authors:

> Betty read her essay on "Why it was morally right and wrong to go to Bea's during furlough." House had disagreements about Betty's essay. It had its good and bad points. Betty seems to be just disregarding furlough rules. A major change

in Betty is going to be up to her. Betty had some feelings about
the essay, but she is going to give it some thought.

Mary talks good in group, and she makes a good effort.
But we'll talk about it some more. House is going to vote on it.

We have a new girl who wants to come here. Phyllis
brought up what the house was going to do about former
members [of the community], parole violators [returned to
prison], who are waiting to come back into house. There are a
lot of mixed feelings about it. Nancy asked why house
members or *staff* haven't been over to see Bobbie. I feel that
staff should go visit Bobbie. She is a former member of this
community, and she needs our moral support.

Betty, a habitual criminal and long-time resident of Niantic,
had violated a standard furlough restriction by visiting a former
inmate (Bea). She insisted the rule was insane for someone like herself
who had no "straight" friends any longer. Others in the group found
the rule objectionable primarily because it was unenforceable. Yet
Betty's attitude toward rules in general was invariably negative. The
community was able to separate and discuss the various claims over a
period of several meetings for Betty's consideration. This is particularly noteworthy, given Betty's former high status in the inmate
subculture.

The community was also concerned about ensuring a high
degree of commitment from new members as witnessed by the tenta-
tive vote of confidence extended Mary, a new member. A great deal of
time was also spent discussing the unit's obligation toward former
members (such as Bobbie) who had returned to prison. Experience
had shown that returnees were often extremely troublesome, and yet
many staff and inmates felt a sense of responsibility.

By July, much of the positive feeling evidenced in April was
absent. Community meetings were usually boring and dealt largely
with trivial matters. An indicator of the tone of the house was the
number of community meetings called because of a cleanliness issue;
in July there were no fewer than eleven notations of the "House being
a mess." The cottage was no dirtier in July than it was in April, but it
was easier to confront the business of a messy pantry than the real
problems facing the house. A July 11th log entry is illustrative:

House meeting called by Sue to make house aware of bathroom not being clean. It turned out to be Bea's assignment, and she was in the infirmary. Point made of covering assignments for girls that are sick. Sue questioned Mary about pull-up [warning] for not cleaning kitchen. Sue eventually accepted pull-up, but states she does not remember Mary telling her about it. The house seems to be aware that there is more to the situation than meets the eye. Sue has stated she has bad feelings toward Mary and at one point called it "hate." A lot of feelings were brought out, but the issue was not resolved due to lack of time.

By August, the cottage meetings were even shorter (two instead of five hours) and more trivial and boring than in July. Staff members had several indications that there was a major division between them and the inmates. Besides discussions of cleanliness, most meetings were concerned with inmates asking for privileges. It also became clear that a small, violent homosexual clique was dominating the program. At one meeting, the one remaining heterosexual inmate in the cottage delivered a farewell speech the evening before her release as follows: "I know that all of you in here dig going with broads. I don't know what it is, but I do *not* dig this girly-girly shit. If I had to do it again, I would not go near this program." Indicative of the character of the cottage population, a moral judgment survey revealed that only three of the eighteen residents were Stage 3 or above, six were more or less chronic "program" addicts (primarily interested in personal comfort and friendship), and several were extremely violent and almost uncontainable in any other setting (one had beaten staff and escaped eight times from other programs, and three others were nearly as difficult).

There also evolved a growing split between staff members on the afternoon and evening staff shifts, with the latter accusing the former of being too soft on the inmates. "It makes it tough on us," one evening staff worker argued, "if the afternoon staff let the women do whatever they please."

By September, the community cracks had become gaps. Tension over homosexual relationships had increased. Overt inmate hostility toward staff also had increased, and four women were disciplined during the month for "cussing out" staff members. Only trivial punishments were dispensed in community meetings. Offenses that ordinarily might have led to expulsion were handled lightly. For example, when an inmate named Lisa called a staff member a strong epithet, she received as punishment only a loss of furlough and the requirement that she write a 200-word essay on "Why I should not cuss." Lisa immediately appealed the penalty as being too harsh. The final signal that all was not well was an escape by two women, Ann and Marge, only the second escape from the cottage in five years. Several of the inmates knew the escape was being planned, and one actually aided it but was only asked to write an essay on "community responsibility." Later it developed Marge had delivered Ann to some male friends, who beat and raped her and "turned her out" on the streets as a prostitute. When one of us asked the group what it thought of Marge's "friendship" with Ann, several women rudely told him to mind his own business!

The calm of April had evolved into near chaos by mid October, with fights involving homosexuality, and community meetings marked by openly negative expressions of feeling. The crisis reached a head on October 18th, when a staff member discovered a narcotics needle in an inmate's room.

In the community meeting, the supervisor stated, "We found a needle [and] a burn spoon with white powder still on it . . . in Gale's room. What are we going to do?" The next hour repeated a scenario replayed many times that summer. Gale, a long-term addict, reacted with mock hurt and surprise: "Mrs. Smith, I don't know where that came from. I never seen that spoon before." Several minutes of mild browbeating produced no confession, and the staff members were near desperation.

The situation worsened when Peggy, who had been Gale's lover, declared to the group that she had put the stuff in Gale's room—a suspect confession because Peggy was to be automatically released the next month, whereas Gale was serving an eight-year sentence and could not afford any more setbacks. Then Jerrie (who was "going with" both Peggy and Gale) announced that she had helped Peggy put the drugs in Gale's room. To top it off, Sue, Connie, and Barb, all close friends of the "indicted" trio, showed strange dilation of the eyes. Another inmate asked them directly, "Is you all high? Right now?" but they seemed apathetic, and barely said a word during the entire meeting. Finally, Gale was exonerated, and Peggy and Jerrie received mild wrist slaps in the form of lost furloughs and required essays. Three staff members left the meeting early, one in tears.

The following day, the unit director called a marathon staff meeting at which the fury among the program's officers was bitterly evident. Three staff threatened to quit immediately, and one announced, "I refuse to be humiliated by these women! I've had it! This is it!" As a last-ditch effort, it was decided to create a form of martial law. The following day, five women—Peggy, Connie, Sue, Alta, and Barb—were expelled from the cottage community. Two weeks later Gale and her new lover Terrie decided that they had had "enough moral development" and voluntarily retired from the program. (Interestingly, Sue, Connie, Alta, and Gale all escaped from their new unit the following month; all were later caught.)

Rules were reformulated by the remaining residents, new inmates were introduced to and socialized into the cottage, and the program was revived. By January, small groups had begun to meet regularly. By February, there was an obvious renewal of the program's sense of community. By March, only one remained from the disastrous fall of 1975. On March 30, 1976, one of the authors wrote in his log that the cottage "had the best group I have seen in Niantic in four years."

Conflict Between Prison Bureaucracy and Inmates

Max Weber was perhaps the first major sociologist to appreciate fully the impact of bureaucratic control on the quality of social life within complex social organizations. Whereas decentralized or feudal-patrimonial institutions were characterized by personal authority and a high degree of organizational autonomy in subunits, Weber stated, bureaucracy had fixed jurisdictions, offices ordered by rules, centralization of control, and an assumed hierarchy controlled by top administrators.

In a bureaucratic prison, rules are enforced throughout almost dogmatically. Guards are bound by the letter of the law and have to operate with a high degree of accountability and control. Cressey (1960) observed a typical orientation speech delivered to new guards as an example of bureaucratic norms in a prison context: "You are here to enforce the rules of the institution. Every rule. You must enforce every rule. If we thought that one of these rules was not needed, we would throw it out. We go over them every now and then and decide whether they should be changed. We did that about five years ago, went over with all of the departments the rules that applied to them. So don't fail to enforce a rule, even if you think it is nonsense. It is there for a reason. Don't blow hot and cold; enforce it."

For Weber, bureaucratization represented, in general, a movement toward greater social justice, for in the public as opposed to private realm, he felt, law becomes a "collective abstraction" rather than the possession of particular officeholders. Thus, duties and obligations referred not to particular persons but to abstract incorporated offices. Weber wrote, "Only with the bureaucratization of the state and of law in general can one see a definite possibility of separating sharply and conceptually an 'objective' legal order from the 'subjective rights' of the individual which it guarantees; of separating 'public' law from 'private' law. Yet it was left to the complete depersonalization of administrative management by bureaucracy and the rational systematization of law to realize the separation of public and private."

The "depersonalization" of justice in the bureaucratic prison clearly serves some positive functions, for justice is removed from the hands of particular individuals and is determined through application of rules. In a bureaucratic prison, for example, inmates are assured of "at least 2,800 calories per day," whereas in a feudal prison they might receive only what the jailer felt like giving them. Bureaucratic public law also means there are common, accepted rules that, in theory, bind both inmates and staff, so that the guard who violates these rules is liable to punishment. Thus, in bureaucratic prisons, the chances of sadistic guards mistreating inmates are greatly reduced through the careful ordering of prison relationships.

No doubt bureaucracy has its social and economic advantages, but Weber ignored some serious dysfunctions, one of them being a form of moral blindness. In the bureaucratic form of organization, "moral" decisions are invariably translated into "technical" decisions. This means that members of the line staff make decisions only about correct applications of rules—they do not question the validity of the rules themselves—and rules are often enforced whether or not they make sense and irrespective of their merit or justice. A second drawback is that since bureaucratic prisons operate without the active cooperation of inmates—that is, with an imposed order—rules may appear logical and reasonable to officials but not to inmates. It is probable that inmates in a lower moral stage of development never understand the abstract logic of the "public law" of bureaucracy. Although administrators may see bureaucracy as the only efficient and rational mode of organization, the inmates only perceive that they are prisoners of unwanted and often unnecessary rules and restrictions. Related to this is the fact that bureaucratically made rules are necessarily designed to manage the troublesome individuals at the expense of the more trustworthy. In an effort to enforce order on the handful of troublemakers, a sort of leveling develops that treats all as untrustworthy. A standard response, for example, to the Just Community program's periodic requests for rule changes was "We can't allow it for one if we can't allow it for everyone." The net effect of this phenomenon on both staff and inmate is to gradually encourage dependence and apathy at the expense of individuality.

Bureaucratic organizational structure often conflicts with "islands" of power within its boundaries. The emphasis on hierarchy, centralization, structuring by rules, and routinization of command makes it difficult for autonomous communities to survive for any periods of time. The creation of rules by autonomous groups conflicts with those created by a central authority. Similarly, the possibility that the autonomous community would create rules different from other units conflicts with the notion of bureaucratic equity.

To understand the tension between the Just Community program and the Connecticut Department of Corrections bureaucracy, let us briefly review the histories of both. When Ellis MacDougall was appointed Connecticut's first corrections commissioner in 1968, there was no organized department of corrections but, rather, loosely federated, autonomous prison units, reformatories, jails, and maximum security facilities under the direct political control of the governor. These units were supervised by a number of political appointees with no visible qualifications for their jobs. As a result, shift captains wielded tremendous administrative power and exerted control by commanding the allegiance of the guards on their shift. The result was that there was often open rivalry and feuding between shifts, jobs were awarded as political favors and often to friends and relatives of those already on the staff. Loyalty was more important than competence. Promotions were often attained through a "ratting" system, in which guards "ratted out" (informed) on superiors and peers.

Commissioner MacDougall immediately placed almost all positions under civil service regulations, replaced the wardens with appointments of his own, and made promotions increasingly conditional on ability and test scores rather than on connections. After these reforms, correctional officers were forced to deal with inmates by strict procedures, and the old system of punishment and control, enforced by physical as well as psychological violence, gave way to a bureaucratic system of discipline. Instead of dealing directly with the inmates themselves, officers wrote up reports, which were acted on by a discipline committee whose decisions were reviewed routinely by "central office." MacDougall also created a suggestion box in which inmates were asked to report "injustices" confidentially to the commissioner's office, thus serving further to police actions taken by guards. The MacDougall reforms, in short, meant the establishment of control by the commissioner, not the guards.

The exception to this scenario was Niantic. Janet York had been appointed superintendent several years before the establishment of the Department of Corrections. A lifelong resident of the Niantic area, her ties to the institution went back to her childhood. Indeed, much of her life was interlaced with it. She had worked on the prison farm during high school. After college and graduate school, she returned as a parole officer and was carefully groomed by her predecessor for the superintendency. She was, in short, the personification of the institution and the very paradigm of Weber's feudal-patrimonial model. Over the years, she had necessarily built a political support system at the local, state, and national levels. Authority, however, was not simply political. She truly was a sagacious administrator dedicated to the social work ideal. And, while crisp, businesslike efficiency was never her strong point, there was absolutely nothing that happened at Niantic of which she was not almost immediately aware. In short, Janet York was an extremely competent, politically powerful administrator. And while she supported the creation of the department of corrections, she also rightly feared that it would initially create a great deal of confusion for her operation, as newly appointed administrators struggled with centralization. Because of Niantic's uniqueness, or rather York's, it was decided that her duties should be expanded to include not only the superintendency of Niantic but also all female offender services throughout the state. She as promoted to a deputy commissioner. Thus, as the centralization took shape elsewhere, under MacDougall's guidance, Niantic adapted to the changes at its own pace while maintaining its traditional posture.

It was this half-world somewhere between a fiefdom and a centralized bureaucracy that we entered in 1971. The Department of Corrections was now under the direction of John R. Manson, who was mandated by a new governor to extend the centralization process, close Niantic, and move the women to a new prison to be built at Cheshire. Niantic, for its part, was by now largely dependent on the central office for all administrative support but was still exercising a good deal of operational autonomy. The riot in the spring of 1971, described in an earlier chapter, convinced everyone that the inevitable marriage could no longer be postponed.

The Just Community project became for a while an acceptable matchmaker. Since our earlier work at Cheshire had been largely negotiated through the commissioner's office, we were viewed as having the commissioner's support. At the same time, we were employed by Harvard University, which gave us a certain autonomy from the inevitable office politics and some much-needed expertise. Thus, for the first time the central office was able to offer a mutually acceptable solution in the aftermath of a major breakdown in Niantic's operation.

However, the existence of the large bureaucratic order of the Department of Corrections created some difficulties for the Just Community program, the principal one being the conflict between the bureaucratic rules created by the department and the democratic rules created by the cottage members. Obviously, this implied a radically different relationship between the model cottage and the larger system than was true of traditional cottages at Niantic.

Whereas in the traditional prison bureaucracy most decisions tended to flow downward from commissioner to superintendent to captain to officer, in the Just Community program the goal was to keep as many decisions as possible at the cottage level. As we observed in Chapter Four, this arrangement was achieved by negotiations among inmates, staff, and administrators so that the cottage was permitted to handle certain actions usually delegated to the bureaucracy; these actions were defined as shown in Table 8. The key term is *permitted.* The bureaucracy, through the Niantic superintendent and the commissioner, permitted the Just Community program the *privilege* of dealing with particular activities. This is not to belittle the powers granted to the program; to an inmate confined in a maximum-security prison they would seem unrealistically overgenerous. However, again and again we confronted the reality that the cottage democracy was a democratic state within a bureaucratic order—in short, a limited democracy.

Table 8. Activities Delegated to Just Community Program and Reserved to Prison Administration.

Just Community Program	*Niantic Administration*
Discipline within units	Class 1 disciplines occurring outside
Disciplines occurring outside of unit and not Class 1 disciplines	of unit—felonies, escape, riots, drugs, and so on
Parole references	Review of furloughs
Inmate selection	Review of parole references
Expulsion of inmates	Review of inmate selection
Recreation activities	
Furlough nominations	

This reality often created severe difficulties. An inmate proposal would be accepted by the Just Community staff and inmates but would be vetoed by the prison bureaucracy. For example, once the men's model cottage voted to establish an honor system whereby responsible inmates would have greater privileges (such as unescorted walks), but the prison superintendent refused to allow it because it was unacceptable from a "security standpoint." Naturally, the inmates felt cheated; as one commented, "They imply that you got a say in here, but it's really Frontstreet [the administration] that decides."

The issue of sex between male and female inmates was especially troubling. Most inmates did not regard heterosexual sex as irresponsible activity, and some even felt it was the prison's "most rehabilitative activity by far." Although many officials privately agreed, the department of corrections did not feel it could accept a rule condoning inmate heterosexual contact. At one point Deputy Commissioner York asked the male unit to create a rule dealing with the problem of sex, but the men refused, on the grounds they could not enforce a rule they did not believe in. Despite the reasonableness of the deputy commissioner, many inmates seemed to feel that in many areas they could not create rules reflecting their most mature consciences, and this led many to believe the program was more a sham than genuine democracy.

The idea that cottage rules could be revoked unilaterally by the administration was especially upsetting to inmates. On two occasions, the Niantic administration refused to allow the cottage to discipline male inmates found having sexual relations with female inmates and, instead, summarily returned the offenders to Cheshire. The decision not to punish obviously carried political risks to the prison system as a whole, and, given his or her institutional role, the superintendent or captain could not give the cottage prerogative to deal with such a serious matter, which might prove dangerous or embarrassing to the larger system. However, this did not make inmates any less bitter. As one complained, "Well, in theory the cottage is supposed to decide things like that. But if [the superintendent] wants to ship them, she can. . . . It's all martial law at the bottom of it." Withholding power from the cottage was most damaging to morale when it occurred *after* the inmates had voted on a particular issue. At one point, when inmates developed an elaborate plan to return violators to Cheshire, the administration, reversing earlier statements, indicated it could not meaningfully approve such a policy.

Besides affecting inmate attitudes, the reality of the larger bureaucracy affected staff morale as well. During one wave of escapes from other units, all cottage officers were required to conduct head counts every two hours, even though none of the escapes were from the Just Community unit. "I don't get it," one staff member remarked. "Either they want us to talk to the guys, or they want us to count them. This is too much!"

Another bureaucratic tension involved the apparent inequity between the model cottage rules and the rules for other cottages, with, at various points, the Just Community rules being laxer or harsher. This disparity led to tension between the substantive justice of the Just Community program and the formal bureaucratic justice of the department of corrections, creating a dilemma for the Niantic administration. As one correctional captain argued, "A woman gets busted for dope down in the Trumbulls [a traditional cottage], she gets ninety days overtime. In your cottage, she gets an essay. Is that fair?" Such dilemmas did not derive simply from ill will or defensiveness among the Niantic staff or the staff of the central office of the department of corrections but were the result of there being a large centralized organization that included autonomous units such as the model cottage programs. Indeed, the fact that the Just Community program survived as long as it did is a credit to the inmates, staff, and administrators willing to endure this ambiguity.

Democracy and Involuntary Servitude

Another factor affecting the attempt to initiate democracy at Niantic was the fact of prisoner's involuntary status. After all, could an inmate be said, in any meaningful sense, to "volunteer" for the Just Community program? Morris, in *Future of Imprisonment* (1974), confronted the issue directly when he distinguished between *facilitative* and *coercive* therapies. Any agreement between the prisoner and his or her captors is obviously different from the bond among natural equals that John Locke and Rousseau envisioned. This dilemma is not restricted to prisons: The failure of democracy in Asia, Latin America, and other areas with unbridgeable economic differences is a testament to the incompatibility of constitutional rule with great differences in wealth and power.

Early enlightenment political theory had assumed that constitutional democracy was not viable because of economic and political inequality. Hobbes ([1651] 1953), for example, believed that natural inequality among men militated against any meaningful sharing of political obligations, that the mass would never be able to rule itself, and that a powerful sovereign magistrate was necessary to prevent the common man from regressing to savagery. Others, such as Hitler, Peron, and Mussolini, have also used this Hobbesian rationale to justify autocracy as necessary to control a violent competitive mass.

Democratic theory, by contrast, sought to establish the potential equality of the ruler with the ruled. For example, John Locke ([1690] 1966) attempted to justify representative constitutional democracy by establishing the ultimate equality of citizens with the magistrate. He did this by postulating a hypothetical state of nature in which equals met and formed a social contract that conceded certain personal rights to the magistrate for the good of all. In exchange for protection, for example, the individual gave the state the right to punish transgressors (but maintained all his natural rights and prerogatives). Fundamental to Locke's theory of democracy was the principle of social equality, for there could be no meaningful social contract, he thought, without substantial equality and freedom among all those contracting, state as well as citizens. In the Just Community experiment, this tension between social inequality and democracy recurred over and over. Democracy requires the consent of equals, but in the prison we could hope for at best only a partially voluntary consent by unequals.

We puzzled about it again and again: Was the social contract that was created during the early months of the project a fiction imposed by us—and supported, of course, by the prison administration? In what sense could it be considered a meaningful agreement between the different social elements involved? It was demonstrated again and again that prisoners are legal, social, and economic unequals within prison. They could not legally enforce discipline against themselves, much less staff members. They certainly could not vote to have a warden or commissioner removed from office. Their right to legally redress grievances was clearly limited. Legal services were restricted or unattainable. As convicted felons, they had lost the civil rights that prison employees still had. Economically, they rarely had the power to enforce their demands such as by striking (no one really cared whether production of state laundry, state signs, or license plates was delayed). Prisoners were divided by an impermeable class or caste barrier: They were *inmates* first, last, and always; staff members were forever "staff." Efforts to reduce this barrier even symbolically were resisted vigorously by staff members and administrators, even some in the Just Community program with its ideological commitment to community and equality.

This social inequality between inmates and staff members haunted the project from its inception. The first constitutional debates in 1971 were conducted in a climate of relatively great equality among inmates, staff members, and administrators. This was one of the outcomes of the 1971 riots: It was clear the inmates had an important commodity to sell—namely, order and cooperation—for riots are costly and embarrassing for administrators. Thus authenticity of these discussions rested on the implied threat of inmate disturbances. However, the later "negotiations" in ensuing marathon meetings lacked this near balance of power.

In one community meeting that demonstrated this inequality between staff and inmates the prisoners complained that we (Hickey and Scharf) and unit director David Konafel had infringed on their rights by creating a parole violation policy without their consent. An articulate, long-time inmate named Jim argued that the inmates should vote democratically "to make the directors of the program dictators." This, he suggested, "would look great to the people in Washington, who gave you all those bucks to play democracy with us." This announcement that we (the staff) had all the power revealed a painful truth: Democracy was a privilege granted by a powerful prison system to the inmates that, like all gifts between unequals, could be unilaterally revoked.

Smith (staff):	I think you men [Hickey, Scharf, and Konafel] were being unfair to the residents, but I think maybe you were feeling that the inmates were not strong enough to handle that kind of decision. . . .
Jim:	I've got a proposal. Let's give Hickey and the rest of them an ultimatum. Unless they give this to us, let's make this a totalitarian state. If it's a matter of will, let's find out who is the stronger.
Smith:	Do you have an attitude, Jim? You mad at Joe?
Jim:	[Ignoring Smith] The real issue is whether Hickey and the rest, Peter Scharf and Konafel . . . have the power to infringe on our democratic power. When they infringe on democratic power, let's kill democracy. Let's put a real bottom line . . . [on it].

Jake:	It won't work, asshole. Then they really have *all* the power. He'll make *all* the decisions. . . .
Jim:	Let's face it. They don't need us.
Baumgartel (staff):	The bottom line isn't Hickey. It's [the administration]. I think Joe can't give you this one.
Jim:	If we don't define in certain terms, then there is no democracy. If we're sincere about democratic society, let's do it. Otherwise, let's just say that's what it is: a regular prison unit.
Jake:	Let's take a vote.
Jim:	I want a bottom line. If no democracy, then no program. Nothing at all. [He states proposal fully.] . . . OK, guys, it's shit or get off the pot. . . . Anyone opposed?
Phil:	Look, man, that's life. They have all the power. . . .
Jake:	We're sick of this shit.
Rich:	I dig what Jim's saying, but look, how would you like it if you were Hickey and a bunch of cons start jumping in his face? He wouldn't dig it too cool. . . . Give him a, you know, graceful out. He don't need us. He'll just ship our asses out. . . . If you jump in his face he'll react. . . .
Phil:	I usually don't buy Rich's bullshit, but he's right. They do not need us. We're *inmates.* We can be *replaced.*

Jim's proposal was defeated by a vote of ten to seven, but the recognition that "We can be replaced" highlighted a harsh reality confronting any movement seeking to democratize prison life. The social contract between prison and prisoners was largely a *convenience* to the prison and might be revoked at the whim or desire of the prison administration. Caught between cautious prison administrators and rebellious prisoners was the line staff of the Just Community project, who at once wished to make democracy viable and at the same time recognized that at best it could only appease both sides. At times seeking to allow the "democratic" group to assert itself, at other times attempting to coerce the group to accommodate itself to the realities of administrative power, they were caught between contradictory pressures that would in time destroy the project. What was surprising was *not* the eventual fall of the project but rather that both the staff and inmates were able to live with the Catch 22 of this strange democracy as long as they did.

The Legal System and Democratic Trust

As with Osborne's Mutual Welfare League, the lack of legal status given the inmate-staff democracy provided a further constraint on the Just Community program's effectiveness. In one incident, for example, the unit supervisor of the men's cottage was told by a group of inmates about the circumstances of a drug-smuggling incident in which a small quantity of marijuana had been brought into the institution. The prison administration referred the case to the state police, who questioned the supervisor. The supervisor asserted that he could not give the police the information they requested, because there was a tradition of confidentiality within the cottage. The state police threatened to indict the supervisor and pressured the department of corrections to order the officer to disclose the information revealed in the meeting.

This issue of the legal status of the program democracy was never fully resolved. Because of the project's informal status within the large correctional bureaucracy, neither inmates nor staff could adequately claim its protection as rights, and so, as in this case, information revealed by an inmate in a meeting *could* be used against the person involved. Interestingly enough, in this instance the inmates showed far more self-direction and grit than did officialdom. They advised their supervisors to give the police the information requested even though it would mean their return to Cheshire as a reward for honesty. Staff members likewise were placed in a professional bind when upholding the agreements of the democratic cottage conflicted with the rules of the department of corrections or with law itself. But inmates in particular placed themselves in a legal double bind: The program had appropriated issues normally handled by the legal system (such as marijuana smuggling), but inmates were asked to accept the Just Community democratic program *knowing* that at any point a politically controversial decision could place them and the staff in the hands of the larger legal system.

The bureaucratic limits on the model cottage democracy, the inmates' lack of real power, and the ambiguous legal status of the program meant that inmates could never fully trust the staff or the legitimacy of the democratic framework. This dilemma of trust recurred again and again throughout the seven years of the program. Would inmates tell they had used drugs on furlough, turned tricks on Main Street, or gone for a joy ride across the state line? Would they reveal that another inmate was thinking about suicide or escape?

The mistrust of staff was not just a symptom of a collective paranoia but rather reflected a somewhat accurate perception by the inmates of the institutional power system and the relationship of the cottage staff to it. Indeed, administrators *did* pressure the staff from time to time to reveal information about inmates, and prisoners aware of this would understandably be hesitant to talk about such things in groups. As a result, the line staff faced many professional tensions in maintaining the cottage constitution. When, for instance, an administrator's candy dish was stolen and guards came to the model cottage to search for it, one of the cottage correctional officers refused to allow them in—because the cottage constitution forbade searches by outsiders—and as a consequence received a damaging reprimand in her personal file. In another incident, mentioned earlier, a cottage supervisor was threatened by the state police with legal action if he did not reveal information gleaned from a cottage meeting involving a drug-smuggling incident. When faced with such pressures, some staff members gave the information only in the vaguest of terms, others approached the superintendent directly with, "Look, we've got a problem. Will you let the cottage deal with it?"

The dilemma for both the model cottage and the department of corrections was that the superintendent, deputy commissioner, and commissioner, as well as the cottage staff, all had the legal right and *obligation* to know what was happening, for to withhold knowledge of contraband or an act of planned violence could mean they could legally be held liable for not reporting a serious felony. Two recent legal cases are pertinent here. In *Tarasoff v. Regents of the University of California,* the university was sued because a staff psychiatrist had failed to warn a victim of impending danger. Told by a patient that he was thinking of killing his ex-girlfriend, the psychiatrist had treated the communication as confidential, but after the patient carried through his threat the woman's parents sued the medical center and were awarded substantial damages. This case, then, sets a legal limit to therapeutic confidentiality when there is a danger of impending violence.

In a parallel case, Ronald Vogel, unit director of a youth detention center in Massachusetts, was indicted by a grand jury for being an accomplice after the fact to murder because he had not reported a confession by a sixteen-year-old youth that he had participated the year before in the murder of three people. Although Vogel was acquitted in a three-week trial, the case points up the ambiguity of the correctional counselor's role as a confidant.

The problem of the legal liability of staff members and administrators becomes acute when we consider the importance within the Just Community program (and other therapeutic prison programs) of encouraging inmates to talk openly about themselves. For most cottage residents, however, this involved talking about the street life, which almost always included violence, drugs, theft, and other such crimes. For example, a young female inmate once told the group, "I was sitting in a Dunkin' Doughnuts, and this dude came over and called me a 'fuckin' spic whore.' My boyfriend came back with a gun, and he wanted to blow the dude away, but he had gone." Had the "dude" stayed around, the authors might have faced a dilemma similar to the one that faced Ronald Vogel. Although the Just Community program demanded trust and authenticity, the requirements of the law and the bureaucracy placed a severe limitation on achieving a community of trust in prison. The extension of democracy in prison must overcome powerful legal and organizational obstacles, and no real change can be achieved without a major reordering of the prison's critical tasks and functions. Without such a commitment, the meaning of reform becomes a kind of hopeless defiance against the present system. In the following chapter, we offer what we believe to be a plausible approach to systematic democratic prison reform.

8

Policy Implications and a Model for Prison Reform

In Chapter One, we described a rather dismal prison scene as representative of the failure of American corrections. We also indicated that from time to time reformers have attempted to apply democratic principles of self-government as a logical alternative to traditional punishment techniques. Much of that chapter is devoted to a review of three interventions that we feel are reasonably representative of the many attempts at prison democratization. Each played a direct role in shaping our own intervention work. Maconochie best stated the fundamental moral bankruptcy of traditional incarceration and rightly pointed to unchecked inmate degradation as a two-edged sword that dehumanized the individual while rendering him or her a social burden. Maconochie's remedies, particularly his task-sentencing concept, from which he developed his mark system, was proven practical and effective as both a management and rehabilitative tool. Osborne's general appreciation of the educational potential of democracy was perhaps his greatest contribution to our work. The various structural components of his model were of immense practical help. But both reformers were of a different time and able to initiate their reforms from positions of considerable official power. We were not. Thus Studt's work helped us conceptualize a small model unit within the larger institution that could meet our research, training, and reformative interests. Chapter One also contains our assertions that past attempts to introduce democratic ideals in the incarcerative process failed primarily for two reasons. First, lacking an adequate theory of democratic learning, past experimenters were ill equipped to understand either the qualitative differences among individuals regarding their perceptions of justice in general or their perceptions of the justice of the institution per se. Second, traditional philosophical justifications for punishing offenders are unable to provide an adequate moral basis for action.

Chapters Two through Six discuss our attempts to address the first set of issues by describing our efforts to apply Kohlberg's theory of moral development in a penal setting. Preliminary data (Chapter Six) suggest that 75 percent of the inmates viewed themselves as authors of the unit rules and perceived the program as fair. Further, these perceptions of fairness can be individually analyzed using Kohlberg's stage typology—thus providing vital insights concerning not only the individuals but also the social dynamics of the self-governing living unit itself. In addition, we were able to demonstrate significant growth among participants in moral reasoning.

We are convinced from this work that the application of self-governing processes in prisons, far from being romantic pipe dreams, provides the best hope for a morally defensible penal system in which the individual is treated not primarily as an instrument to social order but as the very justification for that order; as an end in him- or herself. Further, we believe our work is defensible in practical terms. It seems to us that in the various anecdotes we have recounted one can see the best and the worst of human behavior. We have described the follies of staff, inmates, and interveners. Attempts to coerce community votes, for example, while possibly defensible in Machiavellian terms, receive low marks when measured on Kohlberg's scale. Yet we have also recounted moments of true greatness. And the democracy, as limited as it was, endured in the midst of an autocracy.

Possibly our greatest accomplishment, however, was to help create an atmosphere of trust in which both staff and inmate felt sufficiently comfortable in sharing intensely personal and often potentially explosive issues. Chronic prison problems such as institutional homosexuality and contraband, for example, are rarely if ever openly dealt with in traditional prisons, either out of the inmates' fear of official retaliation at parole time or out of officialdom's fear of public reaction. Thus the central theme of our work seems defensible in moral terms. Prisoners, like humans everywhere, generally respond in morally positive ways, particularly when they perceive their environment as fair and just and when they see that this experience can produce growth in moral terms. Whether this personal growth is beneficial in terms of recidivism is unanswerable at this time, given the limited amount of data we have been able to analyze thus far. We believe it *is* beneficial, however. In any event, we argue, for reasons we develop later in this chapter, that rehabilitative considerations must necessarily be subordinated to a more important consideration: the moral integrity of the prison per se. Just as academe must ultimately rest its legitimacy on the quality and veracity of its instruction, in the hope of contributing to the development of well-informed, mature graduates, so also the prison should first seek to provide an environment perceived by all (inmate, staff, and citizen) to be just and fair. In this way, it can help to legitimize and support what is the primary purpose of a justice system within a democracy; namely, protecting the rights and welfare of its individual citizens. Whether an ex-prisoner who has experienced such an environment still chooses to commit further crime must necessarily be a secondary consideration. This does not mean that efforts at rehabilitation or, for that matter, genuine custodial concerns should be ignored, only that somehow they must be dealt with in an atmosphere perceived to be fair and just.

This brings us to our second point: that traditional philosophical justifications for punishing offenders are unable to provide an adequate moral basis for action. Let us briefly review these justifications and then turn our attention to what we consider to be a more promising approach to the act of social punishment.

Four Justifications for Punishment

For present purposes, we understand social punishment to be an involuntary deprivation of freedom of action, imposed on an individual by a duly authorized court acting within the limits of its authority. This definition is similar to traditional notions but avoids justifying such action from any particular philosophical position. In early times, for example, punishment was justified by vengeance. It was left up to the victims or their kin to seek out the offender and rectify the wrong as they saw fit. The inherent lawlessness of such an individualistic and arbitrary approach gradually gave way to the notion of retribution.

Retributionists tend to agree that violation of the law, whether law is thought to derive from God or humanity, is in itself a moral wrong demanding punishment. If the law tends toward the good, then its violation confounds that good, and thus, it is argued, society has a moral obligation to punish. By insisting that the violation of the law is a moral evil in itself, the retributionists are able to argue that punishment exists as a moral end in itself and should not be subordinated to either the needs of the criminal or the victim. Thus, modern retributionists such as Andrew von Hirsch (1976) and others have argued, following Immanuel Kant ([1787] 1952) that punishment is justified only when a moral wrong occurs, not as a means to an end. The retributive-desert theorists, then, are generally concerned less with deterrence, rehabilitation, or reform than with meting out deserved punishment regardless of the consequences to society, the criminal, or the victim.

The historical counterposition to retributive theory is utilitarian doctrine. At bottom, Utilitarians, following Jeremy Bentham ([1809] 1970), justify punishment by making it instrumental in assuring the common good defined in terms of the sum of the individual welfares: the greatest good for the greatest number. That is, utilitarian doctrine suggests that people who are tempted to misbehave, to trample the rights of others, or to sacrifice public welfare for private gain can be deterred from such conduct by fear of punishment. Additionally, those who do actually violate the law and are punished serve as an example to others. The difficulty with this line of reasoning is that in seeking to achieve the common good it provides no adequate mechanism for recognizing individual welfare. Thus, as Pitirim Sorokin (1947) pointed out, Bentham does not take into account that what brings the greatest happiness to the greatest number of people does not necessarily give happiness to some individuals. Conversely, what gives maximum happiness to some people does not necessarily give the maximum happiness to all. In the case of crime, while it might be in the public interest to deter future wrongful acts by investing the state with the powers to punish, one is hard pressed to see the good derived by the victims by such action. Although they have suffered, in some cases, irretrievable loss, they are now asked to help care for their assailants through taxes. As for the offender, he or she is at the mercy of the utilitarians, because the offender's role is to be an instrument of deterrence. As such, the conditions of incarceration are typically determined by the perceived best interests of the public. In effect, the prisoner is made totally dependent on his or her keepers not only for the conditions of incarceration but indeed his or her very existence.

The fourth rationale for imprisonment to emerge in the past seventy years or so is the notion of individual reform. Building on earlier, religiously inspired notions of penance, the modern reformers justify their effort on various disciplines, including psychiatry, psychology, and vocational or industrial education. While they differ as to which approach or combination of approaches works best, all generally agree that the offender must be allowed to progress at his or her own pace and that the key to this is the indefinite sentence with release contingent on a favorable parole hearing. Irrespective of the practical pros and cons of rehabilitation, it seems clear that the rehabilitative ideal by itself does not provide an adequate justification for the act of punishment. Indeed, it tends to ignore it, by overlooking the destructive realities of confinement as well as the moral and legal issues implicit in the very act of law enforcement.

In summary, then, we are persuaded that, while each of these theories provides a partial justification for punishment, none is universal enough to provide the basis for principled action. Revenge is chiefly concerned with legitimizing the actions of the victim to the exclusion of society and the offender. Similarly, retribution, deterrence, and reform theories emphasize the law, the majority, or the offender, respectively, while ignoring the victim. The net effect is a penal system generally at odds with itself as to its purposes and priorities yet willing to permit the deliberate debasement of literally thousands of individual human beings. What is needed, in our view, is a more comprehensive theory of punishment that not only centrally takes into account the legitimate claims of society in general or maintains the authority of the law but also recognizes and protects the rights of both the victim and offender.

Rawls' "Ideal Agreement" and Prisoner's Rights

To provide an alternative to these theories of punishment, we have attempted to adapt recent theoretical developments in order to develop a working philosophy of corrections that sets philosophically rational moral limits on the act of punishment. In his book *Theory of Justice* (1971), John Rawls of Harvard University differs from utilitarian or retributive notions of social justice in offering the idea that *all* people in society should be treated as moral ends in themselves. As Rawls (1971, p. 180) puts it, "Treating men as ends in themselves implies at the very least treating them in accordance with the principles to which they would consent in an original position of equality. For in this situation men have equal representation as moral persons who regard themselves as ends and the principles they accept will be rationally designed to protect the claims of their person."

Starting with this fundamental assumption, he posits a hypothetical situation in which people are asked to create social arrangements for a future society without knowing which position they will occupy. Rawls asserts (1971, p. 60) that, with this "veil of ignorance," a reasonable person would agree to two principles of action designed to maximize individual freedom in all possible role situations: "First, each person is to have an equal right to the most extensive basic liberty compatible with a similar liberty to others." And (p. 83) "Second, social and economic inequalities are to be arranged so that they are both (1) to the greatest benefit of the least advantaged and (2) attached to offices and positions open to all and generally known to be open to all under conditions of fair equality of opportunity."

The contractual perspective, as articulated by Rawls, allows for the loss of social rights only under clearly specified conditions. Rawls argues that the liberties of a person within the social contract may only be reduced, compared with the liberties of other people, when it is for the good of the least advantaged, considered from the "veil of ignorance" assumption of not knowing what role one will occupy. Rawls expands on this line of reasoning to show that his precepts are the best justification for democracy, because they necessarily place the liberties of the individual as the focal point of issues of justice. Thus, a loss in freedom and, by extension, the imposition of punishment on an offender can only be justified when it can be shown to benefit the least advantaged in a given situation and to do so in such a way as to maintain and assure the offenders' other liberties and opportunities.

Rawls' notion of ideal agreement provides a reasonable calculus for what Norval Morris (1974) calls a "moral limit on punishment." We must determine punishment to what might be agreed to from the original position. That is, (1) we must punish only to the extent that the loss of liberty would be agreeable were one not to know whether one were to be the criminal, the victim, or a member of the general public, and (2) the loss of liberty must be justified as the minimal loss consistent with the maintenance of the same liberty among others.

In short, this conception of justice assumes that rights granted other citizens at large belong to the inmate *unless* society can show them to be incompatible with the welfare of the victim and the common welfare so that any reasonable inmate might agree to their temporary suspension.

Consistent with this view of humanity as a moral end in itself, Rawls delineates an epistemology of justice generally compatible with the rationalist tradition of Locke, Rousseau, Kant, and, more recently, the psychological postulates of Piaget and Kohlberg. From this perspective, morality is not simply the learning of socially acceptable motives or the conformist tendencies formed in early childhood; rather, it is the result of the natural development of innate intellectual and emotional capacities as the person interacts with the environment. Morality also ultimately involves a person's capacity to appreciate the viewpoint of others and to recognize the mutual benefits derived from fair dealings and cooperation. In contrast to Rawls' contractual model, with its insistence on treating the individual as a moral end in him- or herself, the utilitarian tends to demand prisoners' rights be preserved, provided this serves to increase the "greatest good for the greatest number." The rights of the offender, indeed the offender him- or herself, tend to be viewed as means toward other social ends. If maximization of social goods is achieved by a benign prison, this aids rehabilitation. If, however, we find the good is served by harsh exemplary punishments, then utilitarian theory justifies severity and cruelty. Similarly, the issue of victim compensation is considered primarily in terms of the general welfare, with only secondary consideration given to the victim or offender. Traditional prison industries and road gangs, for example, in which the prisoner works for little or no wages and from which his or her victim receives no compensation, are typically defended in terms of the social good.

Additionally, the retributive position in its ideal indicates different levels of severity of punishment determined by the relative moral importance of the laws violated, independent of the effect of this severity on either offender or society. Under the principle of just deserts, a cruel sex offender might receive less humane punishment than would a check forger. This assumes gradients of severity or cruelty of imprisonment that fit the moral wrongness of specific crimes. Assuming that crimes were considered sufficiently morally heinous, the retributive prison might be quite brutal, meting out pain in response to the grievous wrong done by the offender and with little regard for his or her actual needs or those of the victim.

Toward a Democratic Economy in Prison

The stark fact facing the reformer is that democratic justice can never be fully extended to prisoners until a philosophy of punishment similar to the one we have outlined is refined for practical usage. This implies that the purpose of punishment would center primarily around protecting the rights of the least advantaged, as determined from Rawls' veil of ignorance. Following this line of reasoning, it would seem that in general the least-advantaged individual in a specific crime would be the victim, followed by his or her dependents directly affected by whatever loss was sustained. It seems reasonable that the offender would be next in our hierarchy, because his or her personal liberties are at stake, which in Rawls' view are the central purpose of the law. Finally, social and legal welfare issues would be considered. What we are suggesting then is a revision of present punishment practice in order to rectify criminal injustice by deliberately attempting to maintain the sovereignty of the individual as a proper end in itself. The mechanism for doing this would be a punitive system that would restore the victim to his or her prior state as much as possible through money payment made by the offender. It seems appropriate at this point to present a concrete example that can act as a focal point for discussion.

A Property Crime. Imagine that a home has been burglarized, with monetary damage totaling $5,000. After settling insurance claims, the victim experiences a net loss of $1,000. The police subsequently apprehend a suspect who is eventually convicted of ten additional burglaries and twenty claims of larceny. The adjusted claimed property loss for all his misdeeds, after insurance claims are met, totals $10,000. Under our present system, his victims will absorb this cost.

The presentence investigation of the offender ordered by the court describes a nineteen-year-old white male, former state ward, now married, with one infant son. His criminal record is a long history of minor juvenile offenses and incarcerations. He is deficient both academically and vocationally, has no marketable trade, and has never been steadily employed. Both wife and son are receiving welfare payments totaling $4,000 annually.

Under our present system, such an individual will likely receive an indefinite sentence of some seven or eight years, depending on local judicial practice. After two years or so, if he has participated in some rehabilitation programs and has a reasonably "clean" custodial record, he will be paroled. During his confinement, he will typically occupy his days shuffling between the prison industrial system, the school program, and recreation. Because prison industries are legally constrained to assure inefficient production of inferior products, salable only to governmental agencies at noncompetitive prices, he will learn to work as little as possible for a dollar or two a day. In the school program, he might obtain a high school equivalency diploma of uncertain value. Otherwise he will idle away his time in gripe sessions or in sharing past criminal exploits. He will also learn the brutal realities of prison life, including homosexual rape, extortion, beatings, drug usage, and even murder. If he protests, he will be punished and will quickly learn how to "jail" (survive). Indeed, if he is exposed to this treatment long enough he may even begin to accept it as normal.

Harold Garfinkel (1956), a sociologist, in attempting to explain the broader social functions of prison, identified what he calls "degradation ceremonies." His analysis suggests that everything comprising imprisonment, from the inferior work and educational programs through the daily routine of imminent violence, is a manifestation of society's need for moral condemnation. Garfinkel insists that this condemnation process is not in any sense superficial; indeed, it implies a fundamental recasting of the lawbreaker's identity into a lower being. Whether Garfinkel is correct in his assessment or not is clearly a matter for speculation. Do prisoners eventually come to believe they are of a lower order? Our experiences with prisoners such as those we described in Chapter One lead us to answer yes. But if some readers are inclined to dispute our position or even insist that such degradation is proper treatment for criminals, then we suggest that the enormous financial cost of this process is indefensible. In the instant case, for example, the offender's victims absorbed losses totaling $10,000. They will now join society in spending at least twice that amount to maintain the judicial, penal, and welfare system needed to indulge their moral outrage.

Consider the possibilities if, instead of being sentenced on a time basis, our young thief was sentenced to the task of repaying an assessment that reflected the gravity of his crimes. When he had paid the assessment, he would be freed. He would in effect determine the length of his own sentence. Such an assessment would be sufficient to repay his victims with interest and would also include an additional fine to satisfy society's need to punish as well as reduce the cost of court. Additionally, he would be expected to at least partially support himself and his family. Thus, instead of a time sentence, he would be required to repay the $10,000 to his victims, with interest. Mechanically, the court would make the payment immediately after conviction in his behalf. He in turn would repay the court. In addition, he would be required to pay a discretionary fine levied by the judge not to exceed the total amount he had stolen. Finally, if he was incarcerated, board and room charges would be assessed.

It goes without saying that it would be more beneficial if the offender could fulfill the conditions of his task sentence in probation status but because our interest is with prisons we will assume that he has either failed to make payment in probation status or that the courts felt he should be incarcerated, given his past criminal history and severity of the crimes. Since additional expense will be generated by virtue of his incarceration, an additional financial penalty amounting to a nominal room and board charge of $25 per week would be assessed. Parole could be made available at some future time by preestablishing a portioned eligibility amount. For example, in the instant case early release could be granted when 50 percent ($6,000–$7,000, with interest and fines) was repaid. If a partial payment were permitted, the conditions for remaining in parole status would be continued employment and regular payment collected by the employer. If new convictions occurred, the new assessments would simply be added to the old. Thus, all the present options for punishment—fine, probation, incarceration, and parole—remain available but the arbitrariness associated with their present usage is largely reduced, because the major punitive yardstick shifts from judicial discretion to statutorily fixed fines. Similarly, the duration of punishment is largely in the offender's hands.

What we have described thus far is a system based on self-determined task sentencing designed to provide restitution to crime victims. To accomplish this, we recommend a system of punitive fines. Later we argue that in the long run this approach will provide a fairer criminal justice system not only for the victim but for the offender and society as well. We also suggest that such a system will enhance the possibility of implementing democratic ideals within prison by largely overcoming the various constraints discussed in the previous chapter. First, however, let us flesh out our model a bit more.

Clearly, no repayment plan can fully compensate a victim. Anyone who has experienced a simple auto theft or purse snatching, for example, can recall the fear and frustration it generated. The differential impact experienced by victims exposed to similar criminal incidents are unassessable, thus prohibiting exact compensation. Indeed, the very notion of justice, at least in human terms, necessarily implies a compromise arrangement at best. The task, then, is not to restore the victim to exactly the same position he or she was in prior to the crime. Rather, it is to rectify a wrong as much as possible. Toward that end, we suggest that a reasonable restitution payment be determined by the court at the time it performs the presentence investigation.

This assessment would be guided by such factors as the initial amount of loss reported by the victim to the police; the outcome of insurance claims, if any; and information developed during the trial proceedings. In addition to victim compensation, the offender would be required to pay a discretionary fine whose upper limits would be statutorily set and guided by the total amount originally stolen plus court expenses. This amount could only be repaid through task sentencing. The reasons for this stricture should be obvious. First, the court would always wish to encourage the accused to return what he or she has stolen; thus the restitution assessment would be reflected by whatever amount was returned. At the same time, however, enforcement of the law per se requires some sort of punitive assessment independent of the restitution amount. It seems to us that this portion should be structured in rather broad discretionary fashion, in order to address substantive issues. A wealthy person, for example, could simply repay what he or she had stolen, as well as a fine, with little or no difficulty, unless the court was able to levy the punitive assessment payable only through subsequent labor. Similarly, the court might wish to impose a maximum fine on a chronic offender, simply to deter him or her for as long as possible. At the other extreme, an individual such as we described in our example would be unduly punished, it seems to us, simply because of personal and financial status, if the punitive amount of the fine could not be flexible.

Finally, a nominal maintenance charge of $25 per week would be levied on those requiring confinement. Our reasoning behind a nominal charge in lieu of a total charge is primarily practical. In the first place, the real financial cost of imprisonment is virtually impossible to calculate. The usual method employed by prison officials is designed primarily to derive annual operating budgets. In most states, for example, a per capita cost for each institution is derived essentially by totaling the various operating expenses, staff salaries, heating, food, maintenance, and so forth and then dividing by the average census for the facility. By this method, per capita costs can range from $2,000–$3,000 for a high-volume institution such as a jail to $20,000–$30,000 for a low-volume institution such as a women's prison. Clearly, assessing maintenance costs from these figures is morally questionable and practically disastrous, because inmates in high-volume institutions would pay less than those in low-volume facilities. If an average price were charged, the system would likely experience resistance for making one inmate subsidize another's keep. More important, however, is the fact that prisons are tax-free establishments. Many of them encompass hundreds if not thousands of tax-free acres. When this dollar loss is considered, the present practice of incarceration is simply ludicrous. Indeed, one can fairly ask who is really punishing whom? Finally, we are persuaded that, as a practical matter, a nominal fee such as we have suggested (based solely on the actual cost of feeding prisoners per day in Connecticut during 1978) is realistic if restitution, punitive assessments, and partial family maintenance are to be collected.

In the present case, assume the court assessed $10,000 in restitution, as well as $2,000 in interest and fines and $25 per week in board. If the jurisdiction had no provision for parole, it would take three and one half to four years for the offender to earn release at a minimum annual wage of $6,000, assuming he was allowed to pay at the rate of half his salary per year. Under such a system, he could also cut the cost of welfare support to his family by at least 25 percent and defray part of the expense of his upkeep. Additionally, because he would be employed and therefore eligible for health insurance, he would no longer require publicly supported medical and dental care. He would also be able to choose private rehabilitative services under some medical plans if he saw fit. His release, in any event, would not be based on playing the rehabilitation game, as in the current practice. Rather, it would be based on repayment of a debt owed his victims and society through honest labor. He would in a very real sense pay his debt to society. If he felt a need for counseling or therapy, he would be able to pay for the best available and be assured of professional confidentiality. And the therapist would be reasonably certain that the patient had truly volunteered and was properly motivated. The public, in turn, could feel a greater confidence in the social benefits derived from such an arrangement. We should emphasize that the actual length of incarceration could be regulated by instituting a parole component. Under such a system, release would be automatic after a certain predetermined amount was reached. In the present case, for example, parole could be set when half the total assessment was repaid. Under those conditions, release would occur after approximately two years and would continue, provided regular employment and repayment continued.

Is such a sentencing system practical? Do the figures we have presented fairly represent the average property criminal? Does our $12,000 figure approximate the net damage caused by the average felon? In order to answer this, we analyzed some fifty adult prison records of criminals convicted of property crimes in Connecticut. We were able to ascertain that the average felon was convicted of thirteen separate charges. Because the records failed to give a clear picture of the net losses involved in each charge, we generated an average cost of $845 per crime, using the 1977 uniform crime reports presented in Table 9. When these two figures are combined, they yield an average of $10,985 per offender. Admittedly, this is a rough estimate of the net losses experienced by victims, particularly because the uniform crime report is based on complaint reports and therefore does not reflect

Table 9. Average Cost per Crime (Connecticut, 1977).

Type	Number of Offenses	Average Value in Dollars
Robbery		
Highway	172,510	$ 261
Commercial house	54,894	428
Gas station	21,337	217
Chain store	26,587	422
Residence	43,764	575
Bank	3,983	4,858
Miscellaneous	53,966	245
Burglary		
Residence		
Night	651,102	$ 460
Day	728,418	503
Unknown	462,024	522
Other than Residence		
Night	580,749	$ 420
Day	151,085	417
Unknown	258,909	513
Auto theft	896,493	1,992
N = 14	Average = $845.00	

Source: Adapted from Federal Bureau of Investigation, 1978.

insurance claims. If anything, it is an overestimation, thus tending to support our premise that task sentencing is indeed practical.

The Economic Prison

While our task-sentencing scheme seems workable and practical, our present penal system prohibits such an approach. In our discussion of inmate rights in the previous chapter, we noted that prisoners are economically powerless. They are, in effect, economic chattels of the state. Whatever work they perform has historically been viewed as helping defray the cost of incarceration. Hence they receive only a token wage, typically a dollar or so per day. One could see some practical logic in this systematic disenfranchisement if the products of their labor were competitive in quality and price and thus able to generate a profit. As we mentioned earlier, however, they have been rendered noncompetitive through a network of state and federal "use" laws that carefully regulate the sale and distribution of such products nationwide. This practice is justified on the grounds that prison industries threaten private industry and labor because the wage factor does not exist. The net effect is an expensive system of production barred from competing in the marketplace. This practice succeeds in degrading its workers by requiring only a few hours of work a day at a meaningless task for what amounts to a dole.

There is little argument that a prison industries system that competed on the open market using unpaid labor would be totally unacceptable both morally and economically. It would be tantamount to slave labor. At the same time, a make-work system producing inferior goods at noncompetitive prices for token wages is also on morally weak grounds. We propose, therefore, that private enterprise be encouraged to enter the prisons and operate their industrial components. This could be accomplished either by leasing out existing industrial space and equipment in the prison to interested industries or by moving prisoners, in certain cases, to industrial sites. In the latter case, the government would simply provide security for inmates nearing the end of their confinement. Incentives to industry for such a program could take the form of reduced rent or of various tax exemptions on profits or inventories. The feasibility of this proposal was researched in depth by the South Carolina Department of Corrections in 1973. Its study (1973, p. 1) concluded that, through the use of a privately operated prison industries system, the department could provide prisoners with the following: "(1) fair wages for their work . . . wages comparable to those paid by private business for similar work; (2) on-the-job experience in a modern, efficient business operation; [and] (3) meaningful vocational training which instills a skill demanded in the civilian labor market."

The nature of the enterprise would generally follow local demands and skills. In South Carolina, furniture reupholstering and refurbishing and the manufacture of metal office furniture were seen as the two initial industries capable of successful competition. The study cites several benefits accruing to the inmates, the community, the participating industries, and the department of corrections (pp. 8–9):

Inmate Benefits

1. A good, competitive wage.
2. Teaches basic economics . . . allows them to feel the responsibility and accomplishments of working under controlled conditions . . . many for the first time.
3. Instills dignity and pride of accomplishment.
4. Allows for advancement.
5. Teaches a good, technical skill.
6. Increases drastically chances for postconfinement employment.
7. Provides more freedom and comfort.
8. Helps to dispel the "ex-con" image upon release.
9. Helps dissolve the fears of "no place to go" upon release.
10. Instills the benefits of discipline of handling money . . . money management.

Community Benefits

1. Relieves some of the tax burden by making many inmates self-supporting, tax-paying workers.
2. Also decreases the tax responsibilities of the "ordinary" citizen by removing many of the inmates' families from the welfare rolls.
3. Inserts into the labor force of the state experienced, competent, skilled workers.
4. Hopefully, will reduce the number of recidivists.

5. Helps attract additional employers to the state. This not only increases the civilian employment opportunities, but through the multiplier effect of manufacturing operations expands all aspects of South Carolina's economy.

Participating Industries Benefits

1. Provides a new source of labor.
2. Reduces the normal employee turnover rate significantly.
3. Allows for a planned replacement personnel program.
4. Produces trained workers that, upon release, can be utilized in other company plants.
5. Establishes or increases the "good image" of the corporations.
6. Possibly provides cost-reducing operations in the form of lower initial capital outlay (the leasing program) and operating costs (tax breaks).

Department of Corrections Benefits

1. Expands and improves the already good and progressive image of the South Carolina Department of Corrections.
2. Possibly reduces the number of recidivists.
3. Effectively utilizes inmates' talents, capabilities, and time to benefit themselves and society.
4. Possibly reduces overall costs per inmate.
5. The realistic prospects of the rehabilitation of participating inmates.
6. Improves the morale and motivation of inmates.
7. Allows for better direct utilization of educational and vocational programs.

Interestingly, while this report favored a restitution component in principle, the department of corrections chose to set it aside. We quote (p. 7):

What about restitution? It is believed that a pragmatic, workable restitution plan would be a significant advantage for the study concept developed. It would make the program more popular for the public and certainly make it more palatable with the State Legislature. But, to date, no realistic restitution concept applicable to this program has been presented.

For these reasons and the others stated in the basic study, it is recommended that the restitution area be generally accepted as a desirable part of the Correctional Industries Feasibility Study program. But it should not be tied to this program now. The restitution question should be set aside, completely separated from the report plan, and researched and studied in depth, taking into consideration all possible aspects of reactions to, and actions caused by, the various alternative restitution approaches.

Discussions with various people responsible for the study lead us to conclude that the major obstacle to the restitution component was a disinterested court system. As one corrections official put it, "The judiciary told us in effect to butt out, which is too bad, because I know it would work if we could get together on it."

Thus far we have offered a system of punishment that we believe is fairer than existing models because it attempts to rectify harm done to victims while restoring rights and dignity to offenders at minimal cost to the public. By making a prisoner a tax-paying worker, he or she not only assumes the restitutive responsibilities discussed earlier but also acquires the means to control, protect, and exercise constitutional rights as a citizen. In our example concerning medical and dental services, if our young burglar was dissatisfied with treatment provided, he could change doctors or complain to the appropriate authorities. Neither of these options is open to him under the present system. It should also be noted that there would be a savings to the taxpayer, who would no longer have to support extensive prison medical services.

At a different level, the introduction of fair wages within prison would permit the introduction of labor unions as a viable political force for assuring rights. Interestingly, inmate unions are currently prohibited on the grounds that they pose a threat to "proper penological objectives," including security, order, and rehabilitation (*Jones* v. *North Carolina Prisoners Labor Union Inc.* 97 S Ct. 2532, 1977). From our perspective, this decision is fascinating in view of the rapid growth in membership among correctional officer unions in recent years as a result of mandatory collective-bargaining legislation. Connecticut, for example, recently experienced an illegal strike by correctional workers. If ever there was a threat to proper penological objectives, it surely was this event, which affected every jail and prison across the state. Yet the institutions ran without incident, largely because the inmates assumed many of the responsibilities usually assigned to staff.

Three rather ignoble motives for this phenomenon were suggested at the time by veteran correctional people. First, there was the fact that the prisoners stood the greatest chance of being personally harmed if violence erupted. Second, by cooperating, the prisoners were able to embarrass their perennial antagonists. Third, many prisoners feared a general takeover by state police and military personnel. Whatever the actual reasons, our firsthand experience during the strike convinced us that, at least within the framework of an economic prison such as we have described, prisoners are easily capable of exercising tremendous responsibility, including union membership. Under such a format, issues such as wages, working conditions, and employee benefits would be systematically protected. This arrangement suggests several interesting issues, the most dramatic of which is the matter of inmate strikes. One is tempted at first to view this as almost insurmountable. After all, the idea of inmates striking in conventional prisons is tantamount to rioting. This quickly raises images of the prison riot at Attica, New York. From this perspective, the best one seems to be able to suggest is that prisoner unionization would have to occur without strike capability. And, because wages would be vital to the prisoners' chances for freedom in the "economic prison" we suspect that this condition would be generally enforceable. Yet this answer seems to us to be rather superficial, almost tacked on to our industrial proposal; that is, it assumes somehow the prison would continue to function much the same except for heightened industrial activities. This assumption implies, among other things, that inmates and officers would continue their mutual antagonism. It seems doubtful to us that such would be the case. Rather, we suspect that the presence of an industrial component adequate to employ several hundred inmates would generate a very different kind of institution, one in which the level of activity would be raised in all areas. Many enterprises, for instance, would employ three shifts, seven days a week. This would require additional correctional staff and a restructuring of institutional routine to accommodate activities such as recreation, feeding, and visiting. An area likely to experience the most dramatic change, for example, would be vocational and educational activities.

Let us consider our sample prisoner: A major factor in the length of his sentence is his educational and vocational achievement. It seems reasonable to expect a heightened motivation for additional training on the part of our hapless burglar, if it meant an increase in his earning capacity and thus an earlier release. The same argument can be made, of course, for various counseling services. And, like the counseling services that would for the most part be provided through the private sector and paid for by the client, the quality and type of vocational training would be guided by employment requirements, with certification and teaching provided through approved instruction. This arrangement would undoubtedly increase the likelihood for improved employment on his release. Such training would likely be taken during off-duty hours.

The shift in inmate roles from one of degradation and dependency to independence as a wage earner would work a corresponding shift in staff roles. Degradation, in the sense Garfinkel described it, would be extremely difficult if not impossible for an officer to justify, much less enforce against a fellow wage earner. Indeed, the very interdependence of their respective roles, recast as they would be in a penal system based on restitution sentencing, could well lead to a mutual support system, particularly in labor matters. Thus, in the Connecticut officers' strike mentioned earlier, their illegal job action might have been averted and the same ends achieved if it had been understood in advance that, because the inmates' freedom was contingent on steady employment, they would work during a strike but would refrain from performing the correctional officers' duties. This would have placed additional pressure on management to negotiate expeditiously with both parties. The notion of an economic prison, then, seems to us philosophically sound and defensible in practical terms. There remain, however, several rather emotion-laden issues in need of our attention.

Some might challenge our economic prison, for instance, by pointing to the thousands of honest unemployed citizens. Should they not be given preference over criminals? In a moral sense, we find this objection rather difficult to defend if it means that prisoners should be punished for poor employment conditions over which they have no control. We would add, moreover, that prisoners themselves often are victims of unemployment or underemployment prior to incarceration. A survey of inmates in state correctional facilities in 1974, for example, indicated that fully 78 percent earned less than $10,000 in the year prior to arrest. Of these, 55 percent earned less than $6,000 and 5 percent were unemployed. In terms of their occupation level, well over 50 percent were listed as either semiskilled or unskilled (Parisi and others, 1979, p. 628). These arguments notwithstanding, it should be noted that a prison such as we have described would in itself generate a great deal of additional economic activity not only within its walls but in the larger community as well, as a result of increased business for suppliers, handlers, and the like.

Still, there remain the realities of day-to-day business life. Would businesspeople be interested in prison-based enterprises, and would labor unions permit such industries to exist? Extended discussions with several business and labor leaders prompt us to answer affirmatively, with certain qualifications. Management saw no insurmountable problems with profitability but expressed concern about possible government red tape. Tax and rental incentives to attract businesspeople, similar to incentives offered in the South Carolina survey, were suggested to offset these fears.

Labor leaders understandably foresaw problems if nonprison members lost jobs because of the program. And labor and management alike tended to favor development into lost or new market areas to offset these risks. Interestingly, both a leading industrialist and a union leader suggested railbed reconstruction, particularly in the Northeast, as a likely market. They described current railbed conditions as deplorable and cited the negative impact experienced by nearly everyone in the region in terms of higher living expenses, fewer job opportunities, and reduced mass transportation. A major reconstruction project backed with federal money would create hundreds of new skilled and semiskilled jobs in numerous industries and would easily absorb the two or three thousand prisoners involved. In view of the continuing rise in fuel costs, it seemed likely to our interviewees that such a plan would receive public endorsement.

Finally, it seems to us that if indeed American democracy rests, as we are prone to insist, on the twin ideals of individual sovereignty and free enterprise, then certainly our prisons, central as they are to our entire justice system, should reflect these ideals. Clearly they do not, and anything short of a fundamental restructuring such as we have suggested will fail to rid us of this last remnant of our feudalistic past. The issue, then, should not be whether labor and management will support our ideals but, rather, when and how they will take their rightful leadership role. If these ideals are defensible, they should be so in this most central component of our justice system.

Before moving on to a consideration of victimless and violent crimes within our paradigm, we wish to clarify three mechanical aspects of our proposal that practitioners often raise. These include the matter of inmate wages, management, institutional discipline, and treatment of prisoners who refuse to work.

The prospect of collecting money from several hundred prisoners on payday is unrealistic, to say the least. In addition, the management problems implied in allowing thousands of dollars to freely circulate within a prison boggle the mind. We suggest, therefore, that earnings be deposited either with the court or with the correctional agency and then disbursed. Instead of a paycheck, the prisoners would receive a financial statement.

The matter of institutional discipline under the proposed system has also puzzled some practitioners. The usual practice of locking an inmate in segregation for serious disciplinary infractions could easily place his or her job in jeopardy. It seems to us that a system of fines would be eminently fairer and easier to manage. Because a system of this sort would directly bear on sentence duration, one could argue it would measurably improve custodial functions as well.

Lastly, many people have asked us, "What of the prisoner who refuses to work? Would this not foil such a system?" We respond to this by reminding the questioner that we have attempted to evolve a model of imprisonment that permits recognition of the fundamental right of the individual to direct the course of his or her life. To accomplish this, we insist on a self-determined sentence structure, the duration of which would rest largely in the inmate's hands. The role of government under this approach is simply to protect those rights chiefly by assuring that the opportunity is provided for gainful employment. If a person chooses not to exercise his or her rights and concomitant responsibilities, that decision must be respected, and it follows that he or she would simply remain incarcerated. Of course, the prisoner is always free to change his or her mind, at which point work would be available.

Victimless Crimes and Crimes of Violence

Thus far we have purposely limited our discussion to a rather routine property crime in order to present our ideas concerning task sentencing, victim compensation, and the economic prison in a reasonably straightforward fashion. There are, however, various crimes such as drug addiction, prostitution, gambling, and the like where it is extremely difficult, if not impossible, to identify a victim. In general, we would tend to support decriminalization wherever practical. But one can imagine a situation where institutionalization would still be necessary, as in the case of a long-term addict who refused help. In such cases, the court could impose the discretionary fine as it deems appropriate within the confines of statutory regulations.

There remains, however, the problem of the violent offender such as the murderer, the rapist, or the child molester. Surely, no amount of restitution can ever compensate for a lost loved one or reverse the terrible harm done by the rapist or the child molester. Such crimes seem to lie outside of redemption by human compassion, and many suggest that death is the only appropriate response. Still, within Rawls' paradigm, it would seem that our response to the offender should benefit the victims or their survivors as much as possible. As with property crime, exact compensation is clearly impossible. Nevertheless, the family of a murder victim would be generally better served were it to receive financial compensation for the lost loved one. The amount of this compensation should be substantial enough to adequately reflect loss of the victim and social outrage yet sufficiently reasonable to permit repayment by the offender. Thus, a fine of $10 million might satisfy the first two considerations but go uncollected. On the other hand, a fine of $100,000 levied on a twenty-five-year-old murderer could be repaid within thirty years or so and thus help the victim's family reestablish itself.

According to data collected by the U.S. Justice Department in 1974, approximately 58,800 prisoners, or 30 percent of the total inmate population, were serving sentences for crimes against people. These crimes included murder (18 percent), kidnaping (1 percent), sex-related acts (6 percent), and assault (5 percent). While the study does not indicate the age range for this sample, it does reveal that over

75 percent of the general prison population was under thirty-four years of age (Parisi and others, 1979, p. 628). It seems reasonable to assume that figures for the violence-prone group were comparable. With these figures in mind, we offer the following schedule of fines for discussion purposes: (1) *minor* (no permanent damage to victim) $1,000–$25,000 per offense; (2) *moderate* (permanent damage to victim) $25,000–$50,000 per offense; and (3) *major* (death) $50,000–$100,000 per offense. Besides the issue of reasonable repayment and offender age, we have attempted to provide sufficient range within the categories to permit the court to deal with substantive issues surrounding specific crimes. Thus the foiled attempted murder that results in nothing more than a simple assault could still be punishable by up to $25,000 in fines. Yet a death resulting from a sudden quarrel could be distinguished from premeditated murder.

Returning to our sample burglar, let us now add a deliberate felony murder to his litany of offenses. Under these new conditions, he could owe up to $100,000 in addition to the $12,000 already assessed. As before, his murder victim's family would be paid by the court immediately after his conviction, and the offender would then be required to repay up to $112,000 at the rate of $3,000–$4,000 per year. Whether the entire payment would have to be earned in prison would be a question for local legislators to determine.

Certainly the ideas we have been discussing are not entirely new. The South Carolina study cited previously borrowed many of its basic postulates from the work of Kathleen J. Smith (1964). In her book entitled *A Cure for Crime,* Smith, a former prison superintendent, described a self-determined prison sentence system, and in many ways our model is similar. Her rationale, however, focused on crime prevention rather than on matters of penal justice and democracy. Smith reasoned that if offenders were made to repay their victims they would tend to desist from committing future crimes, because it would no longer pay. She also foresaw that crime detection would also improve, because suspects would tend to inform on accomplices in order to avoid repaying the entire amount alone. Similarly, the Minnesota Restitution project reported by Hudson and Galaway (1977) is currently attempting to accomplish, through the extensive use of work release, many of the objectives we have outlined. It remains, however, to confront the fundamental constraints implicit in American prisons by initiating task sentencing and revamping prison industries, consistent with a more adequate theory of punishment as we have suggested.

Democratic Constraints Reexamined

John Rawls insists that his two basic principles quoted earlier in the chapter are essential for the maintenance of any social system in part because they tend to foster respect among participants. We quote Rawls (1971, pp. 178–179):

> Furthermore, the public recognition of the two principles gives greater support to men's self-respect, and this in turn increases the effectiveness of social cooperation. Both effects are reasons for choosing these principles. It is clearly rational for men to secure their self-respect. A sense of their own worth is necessary if they are to pursue their conception of the good with zest and to delight in its fulfillment. Self-respect is not so much a part of any rational plan of life as the sense that one's plan is worth carrying out. Now, our self-respect normally depends upon the respect of others. Unless we feel that our endeavors are honored by them, it is difficult if not impossible for us to maintain the conviction that our ends are worth advancing. Hence for this reason the parties would accept the natural duty of mutual respect, which asks them to treat one another civilly and to be willing to explain the grounds of their actions, especially when the claims of others are overruled. Moreover, one may assume that those who respect themselves are more likely to respect each other and conversely. Self-contempt leads to contempt of others and threatens their good as much as envy does. Self-respect is reciprocally self-supporting.

With this in mind, we now wish to reexamine, in light of our present proposals, the several constraints to prison democracies discussed in Chapter Seven.

The first constraint we identified dealt with the issue of trust as it related to the temporariness of prison life. By its very nature, the traditional prison is meant to discipline and punish. Clearly, whatever philosophical justification one offers does not alter this reality. It is little wonder, therefore, that a system deliberately designed to disrespect its occupants invariably produces mutual hatred and mistrust. Thus, in our description of one crisis-ridden period in our women's unit we recounted a period of disorganization, the causes of which were as much attributable to the moral bankruptcy of the institution as to the individuals involved. Their fixed sentences assured the short-term jailees a certain independence, because only a new charge could keep them imprisoned beyond the release date set by the court. Thus, they were in an excellent position to maintain some control over their confinement; to reject, for example, some officially espoused values. And, unlike the indefinitely sentenced inmates, whose release date was decided by the system, the jail population was free to substitute a counter culture of their own, which they could, in turn, control. Most of these inmates were, to be sure, in desperate need of help. Yet a lifetime of degradation, of not knowing anything but failure and rejection, implies a certain blindness to the notion that things can be different. To expect one in this situation to seek help from a system legally designed to disenfranchise, to humiliate, and to degrade is unrealistic at best.

But, if the prisoners with fixed sentences had a problem, those with indefinite terms were in even greater difficulty. For them, the struggle for identity required the appearance of seeking help while systematically avoiding it. As one inmate once told us, "You gotta learn to give enough to look good for the parole board but not enough to get any overtime." It is this reality, implying as it does a mutual disrespect, that breeds the mistrust and resentment in prisons everywhere.

There were many times, to be sure, when mutual trust and a real sense of community pervaded our units. Often it was attributed to the presence of older, more mature members or of some one with unusual charisma. But fundamental prison reform can never depend totally on chance occurrences. A total reorientation of goals and objectives is needed.

We contend that the implementation of task sentencing is essential to any real reform effort. Placing the responsibility for the duration of their sentences in the prisoners' hands provides the mechanism for a viable system of inmate rights and thereby forces a shift in the relationship between the institution and the prisoners. Because the prisoners would be wage earners with major financial responsibilities bearing on their freedom, prison degradation could extend little further than the loss of physical liberty. Prison routine would necessarily orient to the needs of its private industrial component, and the correctional officer would be responsible for the protection of a vital labor force rather than the custody of a resentful mob.

The goal conflict between the correctional agency and the inmates described in the previous chapter would also shift. Instead of simply providing care and custody, correctional agencies would be required to actively attract and encourage industrial partners sufficient for the needs of the inmate population. This probably implies a major work release component similar to the Minnesota project mentioned earlier and possibly implies satellite living facilities within industrial complexes themselves. In addition, there would be the task of coordinating a very active prison environment oriented around work rather than idleness. The prisoners, for their part, would no longer be idle for hours on end, because their freedom would depend on work. Thus, the traditional disciplinary issues that continually plague prisons would diminish, particularly when confronted with a system of fines designed to slow down release dates.

We don't wish to imply that prisons would become model industrial communities. Our purpose is simply to show that, as a result of task sentencing, both the keepers and the kept would tend to orient around the same general goals. To the extent that this occurred, a cooperative environment could develop, and mistrust and disrespect would diminish. Within this framework, shared decision making would be legitimized, and a type of democracy along the lines of our centralized representative model described in Chapter One could flourish. The difference would be that, whereas traditional inmate council models are ultimately controlled by the institution, inmate representatives in our format would have the protection of a legally constituted body supported by union associations and the courts.

In summary, we have become convinced over the past ten years, as a result of our experiments with prison-based democracy, that a fundamental reordering of prison objectives is necessary for our entire justice system. Our work during these years has brought us to dozens of prisons, giving us a chance to experience firsthand the hopelessness and frustration generated for all associated with them. It is impossible, in our judgment, to defend the democratic ideal, fundamentally founded as it is on the notion of individual rights, while maintaining a prison system more compatible with twelfth-century feudalism than twentieth-century industrial America.

Justice within democracy demands fair treatment to all individual citizens. Our current practice of ignoring the victims of crime while systematically degrading prisoners is stupid at best and destructive of the nation's moral principles at worst. Clearly there is a need for new answers—answers that strike at the very core of the problem. It is toward this end that we have presented what we believe to be a viable alternative prison model, capable of providing a basis for democratic justice within prisons.

References

Anonymous Prison Superintendent. "Remarks on Inmate Self-Determination." *Prison Journal*, 1977, 57, (2), 63.

Baker, J. E. "Inmate Self-Government in Correctional Institutions." In R. Carter, D. Glaser, and T. Wilkins (Eds.), *Correctional Institutions.* (2nd ed.) Philadelphia: Lippincott, 1973a.

Baker, J. E. *The Right to Participate: Inmate Involvement in Prison Administration.* Metuchen, N.J.: Scarecrow Press, 1973b.

Bandura, A. *Principles of Behavior Modification.* New York: Holt, Rinehart & Winston, 1969.

Barry, J. V. *Alexander Maconochie of Norfolk Island.* London: Oxford University Press, 1958.

Bentham, J. *An Introduction to the Principles of Morals and Legislation.* L. H. A. Hart (Ed.). London: Athlone Press, 1970. (Originally published 1809.)

Berne, E. *Games People Play: The Psychology of Human Relationships.* New York: Grove Press, 1964.

Blatt, M., and Kohlberg, L. *Collected Papers on Moral Development and Moral Education.* Cambridge, Mass.: Laboratory of Human Development, Harvard University, 1973.

Bowers, P. E. "Treatment of Criminals." *Journal of Delinquency,* 1920, 5, 157.

Brockaway, Z. R. *Fifty Years of Prison Service.* New York: Charities Publication Committee, 1912.

Brönfenbrenner, U. *Two Worlds of Childhood: U.S. and U.S.S.R.* New York: Russell Sage Foundation, 1970.

191

Clemmer, D. *The Prison Community.* New York: Holt, Rinehart & Winston, 1940.

Colby, A. "Logical Operational Limitations on the Development of Moral Judgment." Unpublished doctoral dissertation, Columbia University, 1973.

Cooley, C. *Human Nature and the Social Order.* New York: Scribner's, 1902.

Cooley, C. *Social Organization: A Study of the Larger Mind.* New York: Scribner's, 1912.

Cressey, D. *The Prison.* Philadelphia: Lippincott, 1960.

Dowell, C. R. "Experiment in Peer Counseling." Unpublished doctoral dissertation, Harvard University, 1972.

Durkheim, E. *Moral Education: A Study in the Theory and Application of the Sociology of Education.* (E. K. Wilson and H. Schnarer, Trans.) New York: Free Press, 1961. (Originally published 1925.)

Durkheim, E. *On Morality and Society.* (R. N. Bellak, Ed.). Chicago: University of Chicago Press, 1973. (Originally published 1917.)

Federal Bureau of Investigation. *FBI Uniform Crime Reports: Crime in the United States, 1977.* Washington, D.C.: U.S. Government Printing Office, 1978.

Fogel, D. *We Are the Living Proof.* Cincinnati, Ohio: Anderson, 1973.

Friedlander, K. *Psychoanalytic Approach to Juvenile Delinquency.* New York: International Universities Press, 1960.

Garfinkel, H. "Conditions of Successful Degradation Ceremonies." *American Journal of Sociology,* 1956, *61,* 420–424. Also in *Prison Within Society,* L. Hazelrigg (Ed.) (New York: Doubleday, 1968; Anchor Books edition, 1969).

George, W. *The Junior Republic: Its History and Ideals.* New York: Appleton-Century-Crofts, 1910.

Giallombardo, R. *Society of Women.* New York: Wiley, 1966.

Gibbs, J. "Opinion Change After Mild and Strong Prohibitions." Unpublished doctoral dissertation, Harvard University, 1972.

Gill, H. "The Prison Labor Problem." *Annals of American Academy of Political and Social Sciences,* 1931, *152,* 83–101.

Gill, H. "The Norfolk State Prison Colony of Massachusetts." *Journal of Criminal Law and Criminology,* 1937, *22,* 389–395.

Goldfarb, R., and Singer, L. *After Conviction.* New York: Simon & Schuster, 1973.

Goldsmith, K. R. "A Critique of Sharing Power in the Total Institution." *Prison Journal*, 1977, *57*, 58.

Haan, N., Smith, M. B., and Block, J. "The Moral Reasoning of Young Adults: Political-Social Behavior, Family Background, and Personality Correlates." *Journal of Personality and Social Psychology*, 1968, *10*, 183–201.

Hampden-Turner, C. *Sane Asylum: Inside the Delancey Street Foundation*. New York: Morrow, 1977.

Helfman, H. M. "Antecedent of Thomas Mott Osborne's Mutual Welfare League in Michigan." *Journal of Criminal Law*, 1950, *40* (5), 597–600.

Hobbes, T. *Leviathan*. New York: Dutton, 1953. (Originally published 1651.)

Hudson, J., and Galaway, B. (Eds.). *Restitution in Criminal Justice: A Critical Assessment of Sanctions*. Lexington, Mass.: Lexington Books, 1977.

Huff, C. R. "The Development and Diffusion of Prisoner's Movements." *Prison Journal*, 1974, *12*, 175–181.

Irwin, J., and Holder, W. "History of the Prisoner's Union." *The Outlaw*, 1973, *2*, 1–3.

Jones, M. *The Therapeutic Community*. New York: Basic Books, 1953.

Kant, I. *The Critique of Pure Reason*. Great Books of the Western World, Vol. 42. Chicago: Encyclopedia Britannica, 1952. (Originally published 1787.)

Kanter, R. M. *Commitment and Community: Communes and Utopias in Sociological Perspective*. Cambridge, Mass.: Harvard University Press, 1972.

Kohlberg, L. "Stage and Sequence: The Cognitive Developmental Approach to Socialization." In D. Goslin (Ed.), *Handbook of Socialization Theory and Research*. Chicago: Rand McNally, 1969.

Kohlberg, L. "From Is to Ought." In T. Mischel (Ed.), *Cognitive Development and Epistemology*. New York: Academic Press, 1971.

Kohlberg, L. "Cognitive-Developmental Approach to Moral Education." *The Humanist*, 1972, pp. 13–31.

Kohlberg, L. "Introduction to Moral Education." In P. Scharf (Ed.),

Readings in Moral Education. Minneapolis, Minn.: Winston Press, 1978.

Kohlberg, L., and Elfenbein, D. "The Development of Moral Judgments Concerning Capital Punishment." *American Journal of Orthopsychiatry,* 1976, *45* (4), 614–640.

Kohlberg, L., and Freundlich, D. "Moral Reasoning and Delinquency." Unpublished paper, Harvard University Laboratory of Human Development, 1972.

Kohlberg, L., Wasserman, E. R., and Richardson, N. "The Just-Community School–The Theory and the Cambridge Cluster School Experiment." In L. Kohlberg (Ed.), *Collected Papers on Moral Development.* Unpublished manuscript, Harvard University, Cambridge, Mass., 1975.

Krebs, R. "Some Relationships Between Moral Judgment, Attention, and Resistance to Temptation." Unpublished doctoral dissertation, University of Chicago, 1967.

Lane, W. D. "Democracy for Law Breakers." *The New Republic,* 1919, *18,* 173.

Lawes, L. *Twenty Thousand Years in Sing Sing.* New York: Yong and Smith, 1932.

Lemos, R. *Hobbes and Locke: Power and Consent.* Athens: University of Georgia Press, 1978.

Lewin, K. *Field Theory in the Social Sciences.* New York: Harper & Row, 1951.

Lickona, T. (Ed.). *Moral Development and Behavior Theory, Research, and Social Issues.* New York: Holt, Rinehart & Winston, 1976.

Locke, J. *Second Treatise of Government.* (3rd. ed.) New York: Barnes & Noble Books, 1966. (Originally published 1690.)

Maconochie, A. *Thoughts on Convict Management.* Adelaide: Australiana Facsimile Editions Libraries Board of South Australia, 1967. (Originally published 1839.)

Makarenko, A. S. *The Road to Life: An Epic of Education.* Moscow: Foreign Language Publishing House, 1951.

Marrero, D. "Spatial Dimensions of Democratic Prison Reform." *Prison Journal,* 1977, *57* (2), 38.

Martinson, R. M. "What Works: Questions and Answers About Prison Reform." *Public Interest,* 1974, *35,* 22.

Mathiesen, T. *The Politics of Abolition*. Scandinavian Studies in Criminology, No. 4. London: Robertson, 1974.

Mead, G. H. *Mind, Self, and Society from the Standpoint of a Social Behaviorist*. Chicago: University of Chicago Press, 1934.

Michels, R. *Political Parties*. Gloucester, Mass.: Peter Smith, 1978. (Originally published 1915.)

Milgram, S. "Behavioral Study in Obedience." *Journal of Abnormal and Social Psychology*, 1963, *67*, 371–378.

Mitford, J. *Kind and Unusual Punishment: The Prison Business*. New York: Knopf, 1973.

Morris, N. *The Future of Imprisonment*. Chicago: University of Chicago Press, 1974.

Mosher, R., and Sullivan, P. "A Developmental Curriculum for Adolescents." In P. Scharf (Ed.), *Readings in Moral Education*. Minneapolis, Minn.: Winston Press, 1978.

Murton, T. *Inmate Participation in Prison Management*. Minneapolis, Minn.: Murton Foundation, 1974.

Murton, T. *The Dilemma of Prison Reform*. New York: Holt, Rinehart & Winston, 1976.

Osborne, T. M. *Society and Prisons*. New Haven: Yale University Press, 1916.

Osborne, T. M. *Prisons and Common Sense*. Philadelphia: Lippincott, 1924.

Parisi, N., and others (Eds.). *Sourcebook of Criminal Justice Statistics*. Washington, D.C.: U.S. Department of Justice, Law Enforcement Assistance Administration, National Criminal Justice Information and Statistics Service, 1979.

Piaget, J. *The Moral Judgment of the Child*. New York: Free Press, 1965. (Originally published, 1932.)

Piaget, J., and Inhelder, B. *Psychology of the Child*. New York: Basic Books, 1960.

Rawls, J. *A Theory of Justice*. Cambridge, Mass.: Harvard University Press, 1971.

Reimer, J. "Moral Reasoning Among Kibbutzim." Unpublished doctoral dissertation, Harvard University, 1977.

Slavson, S. R. *Re-Educating the Delinquent*. New York: Collier, 1961.

Smith, K. *A Cure for Crime*. London: Duckworth, 1964.

Sorokin, P. *Society, Culture, and Personality: Their Structure and Dynamics.* New York: Harper & Row, 1947.

South Carolina Department of Corrections. *Correctional Industries Feasibility Study: Market Research Phase.* Columbia, S.C.: South Carolina Department of Corrections, 1973.

Stastny, C. T., and Stastny, G. I. "The Changing Political Culture of a Total Institution: The Case of Walla Walla." *Prison Journal,* 1977, *57* (2), 43–55.

Studt, E., Messinger, S. L., and Wilson, T. P. *C-Unit Search for Community in Prison.* New York: Russell Sage Foundation, 1968.

Sutherland, C. E. *Principles of Criminology.* Philadelphia: Lippincott, 1939.

Sykes, G. M. *The Society of Captives: A Study of a Maximum Security Prison.* Princeton, N.J.: Princeton University Press, 1958.

Szasz, T. *Law, Liberty, and Psychiatry.* New York: Macmillan, 1963.

Tannenbaum, F. *Osborne of Sing Sing.* Chapel Hill: University of North Carolina Press, 1933.

Tarasoff v. Regents of the University of California. 17 C 3d 425, 1976.

Thrower, J. "Effects of Orphanage and Foster Care on Development of Moral Judgment." Unpublished doctoral dissertation, Harvard University, 1971.

Von Hirsch, A. *Doing Justice: The Choice of Punishment.* New York: Hill and Wang, 1976.

Ward, D., and Kassebaum, L. *Women's Prison.* New York: Holt, Rinehart & Winston, 1960.

Weber, M. *Max Weber.* C. W. Mills and H. H. Gerth (Eds.) New York: Oxford University Press, 1948.

Wicker, T. *A Time to Die.* New York: Ballantine, 1974.

Index

197